English for academic study:

Speaking & Pronunciation

Course Book

Joan McCormack, Sebastian Watkins,
Jonathan Smith, and Annette Margolis

Credits

Acknowledgements

Published by
Garnet Publishing Ltd.
8 Southern Court
South Street
Reading RG1 4QS, UK

ISBN: 978 1 85964 569 7

A catalogue record for this book is available from The Library of Congress.

Production
Project manager: Simone Davies
Project consultant: Rod Webb
Editorial team: Penny Analytis, Jo Caulkett,
                    Emily Clarke, James Croft, Chris Gough,
                    Fiona McGarry, Richard Peacock,
                    Nicky Platt
American English
adaptation: Jennifer Allen, Arley Gray
Art director: Mike Hinks
Design and layout: Sarah Church, Neil Collier, Nick Asher
Illustration: Nick Asher
Photography: Corbis, David Lyons/Alamy,
                    Jonathan Smith
Audio: Paul Rubens Productions, New York

Every effort has been made to trace copyright holders and we apologize in advance for any unintentional omissions. We will be happy to insert the appropriate acknowledgements in any subsequent editions.

Printed and bound in Lebanon by International Press: interpress@int-press.com

The authors and publisher wish to thank the following people or groups for permitting us to use or adapt their material for use in *EAS: Speaking & Pronunciation*.

Author unknown. (2004, August 15). Men want to be househusbands. Retrieved May 15, 2005, from http://www.uominicasalinghi.it/index.asp?pg=1030.

Garrat, B. and Francis, D. (1994). *Managing Your Own Career*. HarperCollins Publisher Ltd.

Gerhardt, S. (2004, July 24). Cradle of Civilisation. *The Guardian*.

Hoare, S. (2003, August 26). E for Degree. *The Guardian*.

Woolfenden, J. (1990). *How to Study and Live in Britain*. Northcote House.

Woodward, W. (2003, February 22). Affluent but anxious and alienated. *The Guardian*.

Article on page 75 from Newsweek, 29th January, 2009 © 2010 Newsweek, Inc. All rights reserved. Used by permission and protected by the Copyright Laws of the United States. The printing, copying, redistribution, or retransmission of the Material without express written permission is prohibited.

Articles on pages 78, 83 and 84 reprinted with kind permission of *USA Today*, a division of Gannett Co., Inc.

Articles on pages 79 and 90 reprinted with kind permission of *The Washington Times*, LLC.

Articles on pages 80/81 and 93/94 reprinted with kind permission of Time Inc.

Article on page 82 reprinted with kind permission of *The Washington Post*.

Article on pages 91 and 92 reprinted with kind permission of Lynn Lofton.

The authors would like to add the following thanks.

Bruce Howell for materials and advice on Unit 6.

Anne Pallant, Bruce Howell, Colin Campbell, Frances Watkins for suggestions, comments and proofreading of early versions.

Chia Ling Lin (Kate), who gave feedback on trialing the materials.

Introduction

This book combines the important academic skill of speaking with the study of pronunciation, on the basis that both are essential components of communicating clearly and effectively in an academic environment. The Speaking and Pronunciation sections of the book can be studied independently, or they can be combined as part of an integrated program of study.

Speaking: Activities focus on the skills you will need to participate in academic classes and discussions, and will help you develop good presentation skills. (See also the introduction to the Speaking section on page 11.)

Unit topics include:
• Developing a presentation
• Participating in a discussion
• Anticipating arguments before a discussion
• Using a text to support ideas
• Presenting information from charts
• Leading a class
• Finding a focus for a presentation
• Designing a questionnaire
• Participating in a debate
• Presenting a research proposal

Pronunciation: Learning the phonemic alphabet, improving your listening micro-skills and targeted pronunciation practice will help you to develop your pronunciation in English to a level that will enable the listener to understand you with ease. (See also the introduction to the Pronunciation section on pages 137–138.)

Unit topics include:
• Vowel sounds, word stress, and weak forms
• Vowel sounds and word stress patterns
• Consonant sounds and sentence stress
• Consonant sounds and word stress on two-syllable words
• Diphthongs and sounds in connected speech
• Consonant clusters and tone units
• Diphthongs and tone units
• Consonant clusters and intonation

The book is organized as follows.

Contents
Speaking

Pronunciation

Book Map
Speaking

	Topic	Skills focus	Language focus
1	Communicating in Academic Situations	• Delivering a presentation	• Reporting back on a discussion • Agreeing and disagreeing • Using signpost expressions
2	Classes and Discussions	• Recognizing different perspectives • Reaching a balanced conclusion	• Comparing perspectives • Summarizing the outcome of a discussion • Chairing a discussion
3	Examining Underlying Assumptions	• Presenting information from an article • Anticipating arguments before a discussion	• Referring to an article • Exchanging opinions
4	Reading into Speaking	• Using a text to support your ideas • Listening actively • Exchanging information (1)	• Clarifying and confirming understanding
5	The Use of Data	• Presenting information from charts • Building on what others have said	• Referring to data • Referring to what previous speakers have said
6	Consolidation Unit	• Leading a class	• Review and consolidation
7	Supporting Your Point of View	• Finding a focus for a presentation • Preparing for a discussion by thinking the issues through	• Taking turns in a discussion
8	Collecting and Presenting Data	• Designing a questionnaire • Participating in a debate	• Expressing quantity
9	Thinking Rationally	• Presenting a research proposal	• Expressing doubt and belief
10	The Importance of Reflection	• Exchanging information (2)	• Review and consolidation

Pronunciation

	Topic	Objectives
1	• Vowel sounds: /æ/, /e/, /ɪ/, /ɑː/, /ɜː/, /iː/ • Syllables and word stress • Weak forms in function words	• Learn which phonemic symbols represent certain vowel sounds • Practice recognizing and producing these vowel sounds • Learn about the concepts of the syllable and word stress • Practice producing words with the correct word stress • Practice recognizing weak forms of function words when listening
2	• Vowel sounds: /ɒ/, /ʌ/, /ə/, /ʊ/, /ɔː/, /uː/ • Unstressed syllables and word stress patterns	• Learn which phonemic symbols represent the other vowel sounds • Practice recognizing and producing these vowel sounds • Learn more about which syllable is stressed in some types of word
3	• Voiced and unvoiced consonants • Consonant sounds: /θ/, /ð/, /t/, /s/ • Sentence stress	• Learn about the pronunciation of voiced and unvoiced consonants • Practice recognizing and producing these sounds • Learn to identify stressed words in sentences • Practice using sentence stress to highlight important information
4	• Consonant sounds: /ʒ/, /v/, /j/, /ʃ/, /tʃ/, /dʒ/ • Word stress on two-syllable words	• Learn more phonemic symbols representing consonant sounds • Practice recognizing and producing these consonant sounds • Learn where to place the stress in words with two syllables
5	• Diphthongs: /aɪ/, /oʊ/, /eɪ/ • Sounds in connected speech: linking, insertion	• Learn which phonemic symbols represent certain diphthongs • Practice recognizing and producing diphthongs • Learn how the pronunciation of words is affected by their context in connected speech
6	• Consonant clusters: at the beginning and in the middle of words • Sounds in connected speech: disappearing sounds, contractions • Tone units	• Learn how to pronounce groups of consonants (consonant clusters) at the beginning and in the middle of words • Learn how to divide up connected speech into tone units
7	• Diphthongs: /aʊ/, /eə/, /ɪə/, /ɔɪ/ • Sentence stress and tone units	• Learn which phonemic symbols represent other diphthongs • Practice recognizing and producing these diphthongs • Have more practice identifying sentence stress and tone units
8	• Consonant clusters: at the end of words and across two words • Intonation	• Learn how to pronounce consonant clusters at the end of words and across two words • Learn how intonation is used to organize and emphasize information

Speaking

Introduction

1. Aims of the course

The purpose of this book is to help you develop the speaking skills you need to participate effectively in academic classes and discussions, as well as to help you develop effective presentation skills.

2. Structure of the course

- **Organization:** There are ten units in the book. Each of the units is topic-based, e.g., *A healthy lifestyle*, *The world of work*. The discussions and the presentations you make are related to the topic of each unit. The written or listening texts are designed to give you different perspectives on a topic, and also to help you give evidence to support your ideas, thus giving you practice in one of the essential features of academic life.

Units 1–5 are the core units. Each of these units covers aspects of both class skills and presentation skills.

Unit 6 is a consolidation unit where you have the opportunity to put all these skills into practice by organizing your own classes and discussions, and choosing your own topics. (Depending on the course you are taking, your professor may decide that you begin these classes earlier.)

Units 7–10 give you further practice in these skills.

- **Unit summary:** Each unit is followed by a unit summary, giving you the opportunity to reflect on what you have learned.

- **Useful language:** Each unit has a section on useful language—language related to the task you need to perform in each unit. You should try to use this language in the appropriate situations.

- **Student's diary:** The student's diary is a section at the end of each unit. The purpose of this is to get you to think about the process of learning, and the particular strategies you are developing. Having this awareness will help you to be more in control of developing your language skills.

3. Working with the course

When you are speaking in another language, you need to think of ideas and the language you need to express those ideas. This can be challenging. The book helps you with this in two ways:

- In many discussion activities in this book, you are asked to think about and prepare what you are going to say. This can improve your performance. As you become more confident and competent in speaking in English, the need for preparation time should decrease.

- As it can be difficult to concentrate on both ideas and language, you are sometimes asked to focus on the ideas you want to express on a topic, and to discuss these. After the discussion, you are asked to look at, and sometimes practice, relevant useful language phrases (see above). Following this, you are required to return to the original topic, or a similar one, and discuss it again with different students, this time using the useful language.

What you put into the course will determine how much you get out of it. Obviously, if you want to improve your speaking, it is essential that you practice this skill, and you should prepare well for the sessions in class, as well as participating actively in them.

1 Communicating in Academic Situations
Being a successful student

In this unit you will:
- reflect on your experience of speaking in an academic context;
- analyze your strengths and weaknesses in speaking;
- identify and practise language for agreeing and disagreeing;
- consider aspects of a successful presentation;
- give a short informal mini-presentation.

There are a number of different situations in which you will need to communicate orally in English on your academic courses. The main situations are presentations, classes, and discussions. In academic culture, students need to express their views clearly on different issues related to their subject area. These views are often based on a critical reading and evaluation of written texts. The more you study and engage with your subject area, the more your ideas will develop and change. This will help you to develop your critical thinking skills, which are a key part of academic study. It is also important that you develop the language skills that will enable you to express your ideas most effectively.

Task 1: Your experience of speaking English

1.1 **Look at the following list of situations which require you to speak on academic courses. Which situations have you experienced either in your own language or in English? Put a check (✓) in the appropriate box.**

		English	Own language
a	Giving a formal presentation.		
b	Participating in a class (group discussion).		
c	Leading a class (group discussion).		
d	Discussing and giving your opinion in a class on pre-assigned articles you have read.		
e	Speaking with an academic advisor in a one-on-one advising session, e.g., about an essay plan.		
f	Discussing feedback on your written work with a tutor in a tutoring session.		
g	Discussing your studies with other students.		
h	Other? (Please state.)		

1.2 Compare your experiences with a partner using your answers to Ex 1.1. Give details of:

  a) where you had each experience;

  b) how it was organized, e.g., how many students were involved and how long the speaking turns were;

  c) what kinds of topics you covered.

1.3 Discuss your attitude to the situations in Ex 1.1. Which ones do you find, or think you will find, the most difficult to do in English? Can you say why?

This course will help you develop the confidence and the skills necessary to participate effectively in the academic situations outlined in Ex 1.1.

Task 2: Your attitude to speaking English

2.1 Look at the following statements. Do you agree or disagree with them? Which statements are important to you?

  a) I want to speak English with a perfect native-speaker accent.

  b) I want to speak English without a single grammatical mistake.

  c) I feel as though I am a different person when I speak English.

  d) My pronunciation is not as important as grammatical accuracy.

  e) If I can communicate my meaning effectively, it does not matter if I make mistakes.

  f) I don't like working in groups during English lessons because I may learn incorrect English from my classmates.

  g) I want to speak English for social reasons as well as for academic reasons.

2.2 In groups, discuss each statement from Ex 2.1. Appoint one student to note which statements are the most controversial for your group, i.e., which statements caused the most disagreement.

2.3 🎧 1 Listen to another group of students reporting back on their discussion of the points in Ex 2.1. Which statements do they refer to?

2.4 The following words were used in the recording in Ex 2.3. Mark the stress.

Example: co'mmunicate

> discussion   controversial   disagreement   provoke

2.5 Report back to the class on the most interesting/controversial points from your discussion in Ex 2.2.

Useful language: Reporting back

Our group thought the most controversial point was …

Point X provoked the most discussion.

Point X was the most controversial point.

There was some disagreement about point X.

Task 3: Agreeing and disagreeing

3.1 **Read the following statements. Do you agree (A), disagree (D) or partly agree (P) with each one?**

a) _____ If you want to succeed at university, you really need to manage your time well.

b) _____ It's important to do a lot of reading around before you choose a focus for your essays.

c) _____ The best time to revise for exams is just before the exam, when the pressure is on.

d) _____ The same study skills are necessary on both undergraduate and graduate courses.

e) _____ If you've completed an academic course in one country, you should be able to cope with a course in another country.

f) _____ People have different learning styles. It helps you learn more quickly if you're aware of how you learn best.

3.2 🎧 2 **Listen to two students discussing these statements. Does the second speaker agree, disagree or partly agree with each statement? Underline the correct alternate in the *opinion* column below.**

	Opinion	Useful language
a	agree/disagree/partly agree	
b	agree/disagree/partly agree	
c	agree/disagree/partly agree	
d	agree/disagree/partly agree	
e	agree/disagree/partly agree	
f	agree/disagree/partly agree	

3.3 🎧 2 **Listen to the discussion again.**

a) In the *Useful language* column above, write down the exact words the second speaker uses to agree, disagree or partly agree.

b) Try to say the phrases as they are pronounced in the recording.

3.4 **Look at the statements in Ex 3.1 again. Work with a partner as follows:**

Student A: Read a statement.

Student B: Respond, using one of the *Useful language* phrases from the table in Ex 3.2.

Give your own opinion and a supporting reason.

Task 4: Study skills for success

You are going to hear a conversation between two students, discussing the challenges of studying at university. The female student is a native speaker of English. The male student is an international student who studied on an ESL course.

4.1 ☉ 3 **Listen and number the points below according to the order in which the students discuss them.**

a) _____ Plan ahead and begin working early.

b) _____ Choose areas to study that you are interested in.

c) _____ Find out what is important on your reading list.

d) _____ Ask a peer to read your work before submitting it.

e) _____ Use reading strategies to help you read quickly.

f) _____ Deal with stress by finding time for relaxation.

4.2 **Think of your own study suggestions to add to those mentioned in the recording, and write them below.**

a) _____

_____

b) _____

_____

Task 5: Prioritizing study skills

5.1 **In groups, discuss the study skills you will need at university.**

a) Come to an agreement on the study skills your group thinks are the most important for success at university.

b) Now list your choice of the five most important skills.

Build on the ideas from Ex 4.1. Make sure you are able to justify your choice. Remember to use the language for agreeing and disagreeing from Task 3.

Presentation skill: When giving a presentation, you need to help your audience follow your presentation by using *signpost language*. You also need to deliver your presentation clearly. Tasks 6 and 7 deal with these aspects of presentations.

Task 6: Tips for successful study—a mini-presentation

Now that you have looked at various aspects of being successful as a student, consider what advice would be useful for new students. You will give a mini-presentation to the class, explaining why the tips you chose in Task 5 are important.

6.1 **You are now going to start preparing your presentation, thinking about signposting language you could use.**

a) Write your five points from Task 5 on a poster, PowerPoint slide, or OHT. Use key words, not whole sentences. You need to identify the key words for each of your tips for study.

b) 🎧 4 Now listen to a student presenting his top five study tips. Are any of the points the same as yours?

c) Look at the *Useful language* expressions from the recording. These expressions signal when you are moving from one point to another. Use them in your presentation.

Useful language: Signpost expressions

There are five main points that we consider important for successful study.

Our first point is …

Next …

Moving on to our third point, …

Fourth, we think …

And finally, our last point is …

Presentation skill: Signpost expressions are important for:

● opening a presentation;

● guiding an audience through the main points;

● helping an audience understand the organization;

● closing a presentation.

See Appendix 1 for a more extensive list of signpost expressions.

6.2 **Now think about how you will deliver your presentation. Look at the following list of important aspects in delivering a presentation clearly.**

● pronunciation of sounds and words

● intonation

● volume

● speed

● eye contact

Study tip

There are many skills involved in a successful presentation. These include: language, pronunciation, organization and style of delivery.

Presentation skill: The delivery of your presentation is of equal importance as the content. If your audience cannot understand what you are saying, e.g., because your pronunciation is poor or because you speak too fast, then the content is wasted.

6.3 In your group, discuss the organization of your presentation.

a) Decide who will give the presentation; either one group member or two or more group members.

b) Practice the presentation, focusing on the points in Task 6.2. Your group should give you feedback on these areas, e.g., *You need to make more eye contact with the audience.*

Presentation skill: Presentation skills develop with practice, so you will not do everything perfectly from the beginning. Listen carefully to group feedback, as it will help you improve.

6.4 Give your presentation to the class.

Complete a presentation assessment form (Appendix 9a) for each presentation. At the end of each presentation, compare your assessment forms in groups.

6.5 At the end of all the presentations, give each presenter the assessment form you completed for their presentation.

a) Read and think about the feedback you receive from other students.

b) Decide as a class which presentation was the best according to the criteria on the assessment form.

Task 7: A successful presentation

7.1 Think about the following points related to the delivery of a presentation. Which would you consider appropriate or inappropriate, and which depend on the presentation? Check (✓) the relevant box.

	Presentation skill	Appropriate	It depends	Inappropriate
a	The presenter puts as much information as possible on each slide.			
b	The presenter uses color and sound to liven up her/his slides.			
c	The presenter reads from a script.			
d	The presenter memorizes a script and recites it.			
e	The presenter uses notes.			
f	The presenter pauses after each main point.			
g	The presenter reads all the information on the slide.			
h	The presenter stands in one place all the time.			
i	The presenter speaks at the same speed all the time.			

7.2 **In groups, discuss your completed table.**

Task 8: Review

Research into language learning has shown that reflecting on the process of learning has a strong impact on its effectiveness. One way of doing this is through keeping a diary. Either this can be private, or you can share its contents with the instructor.

Before you fill in your first diary entry, complete a self-assessment questionnaire on your speaking skills.

8.1 **Look at the following range of speaking skills. Indicate which of these you feel to be easy or difficult for you (5 = I can do this well; 1 = I do not feel competent at all). Put a check (✓) in the appropriate box.**

Speaking skill	1	2	3	4	5
I can speak accurately, without making too many grammatical mistakes.					
I can speak without hesitating too much.					
I can find ways to communicate my meaning, even if I cannot find exactly the right words.					
I can usually find the words I need to say what I want.					
Most people can understand my pronunciation.					
I can speak confidently in front of an audience.					
I can contribute effectively in group discussions.					
I can talk confidently in my own subject area.					

8.2 **Read the student's diary questions and example diary entry below.**

Student's diary

- What areas of speaking English do you feel you need to work on?
- What can you do to improve in these areas, either inside or outside the classroom?
- How do you feel about the speaking you have done so far in the lessons on this course?
- Remember that thinking or reflecting on how you learn can improve the learning process.

Student's diary July 3

I think my main problem in speaking is my pronunciation and my limited vocabulary. I also feel very nervous when speaking in front of the class.
I did a presentation on good study skills in the speaking class and was really worried before I spoke. I think I need to do more practice of this type, so that I get more confidence. I also need to spend more time practicing individual sounds—maybe I could do this in the learning center ...

Make an entry in your student's diary, answering the questions. Think about your strengths and weaknesses in speaking English as identified in the self-assessment form in Ex 8.1.

Unit Summary

In this unit you have looked at the speaking skills you need in academic situations and thought about your own strengths and weaknesses.

1 **Complete the sentences below in any way you want so that they are true for you.**

a) I find speaking in English difficult when _____

_____

_____

b) I find using English at university can be different from other situations. I think it is important

to be able to speak _____ but some people feel

_____

_____

c) I agree with others in the class that _____

_____

2 **Think about the discussions you have had while working on this unit. Discuss the following questions and agree on a suitable answer for each one.**

a) To what extent did other students agree in the discussion in Task 2 about attitudes to English?

b) Which discussion statement in Ex 2.1 about study skills did students find most controversial?

c) What do you think are the key points to remember when giving a presentation?

For web resources relevant to this unit, see:
· **www.englishforacademicstudy.com/us/student/speaking/links**

These weblinks will provide you with further practice for becoming a successful speaker of English, as well as useful study tips.

2 Classes and Discussions
Learning online

In this unit you will:
- identify characteristics of successful participation in discussions and seminars;
- consider problematic issues from different perspectives;
- practise summarizing the outcome of a discussion;
- examine the role of a chairperson in a discussion.

On your future academic course you will need to participate in classes and discussions with groups of other students. Usually you are expected to have done some preparation, e.g., read an article. These classes take various formats. Some are led by tutors and others are led by students. In these classes, you need to be able to state your viewpoint clearly and to develop the confidence to do this. This course will give you practice in participating in classes, as well as giving you the opportunity to lead one.

Class skill: It is important to think about how you can contribute effectively to a class.
The purpose of Task 1 is to start you thinking about how you can do this.

Task 1: A successful participant in group discussions

1.1 **Decide whether the statements below are characteristics of good or poor class participants.**

a) Put a check (✓) in the appropriate box.

b) Prepare a list of reasons for your answers; if your answer is "it depends", be prepared to explain further.

	The participant ...	Good	It depends	Poor
a	listens to what others say and builds on this, adding his/her opinion.			
b	tries to get other people to change their mind and agree with his/her opinion.			
c	always agrees with other people's opinions.			
d	does not say anything at all.			
e	explains his/her point in great detail, and at great length.			
f	explains his/her points briefly.			
g	is nervous about speaking, but makes himself/herself do it.			
h	encourages others to speak, inviting them into the discussion.			
i	only speaks when asked.			
j	asks other students to clarify what they mean, or to explain further.			
k	changes his/her opinion during the discussion.			

1.2 Compare and discuss your answers with a partner, explaining the reasons for your choices.

1.3 Reflect on factors affecting group discussions in different cultures.

a) What is considered good behavior in group discussions in your own country?

b) Do you think there are any differences from an English-speaking country?

c) If you have experience of different English-speaking countries, do you feel there are differences between any of them?

Task 2: Different perspectives on an issue

2.1 Look at this statement concerning education and consider it from the perspectives of the different people involved (a–g).

> A seriously disruptive child should be excluded permanently from school.

a) the teacher of the child

b) the parents of the child

c) the principal of the child's school

d) the child

e) the child's classmates

f) a child psychologist

g) the education authorities

Study tip

In academic study, you need to look at issues from different perspectives and to think beyond your own experience or position. This is part of the process of reaching a balanced conclusion.

2.2 Compare and discuss your ideas with your partner, giving reasons for the view of each person. Use some of the *Useful language* expressions for comparing perspectives.

> **Useful language:** Comparing perspectives
>
> *From (a teacher's) perspective, …*
>
> *From the point of view of (the parents), …*
>
> *If I were (the principal of the child's school), I'd probably feel that …*
>
> *(The child psychologist) would argue that …*

2.3 🎧 5 Now listen to a student comparing different perspectives on the statement in Ex 2.1. What does the speaker say about the views of those involved?

Task 3: Reaching a balanced conclusion

3.1 **Look at the following statements about school education. Consider each statement from the perspective of three or four different people who might be affected. Consider:**

a) how they would view the issue;

b) the long- and short-term implications of the statements.

In addition to the people mentioned in Ex 2.1, think about the viewpoints of other sectors of society, such as young people, employers, and society as a whole.

> • Corporal punishment is necessary to maintain discipline.
> • Children should be given formal tests and exams from the age of six.
> • Children should be allowed to leave school at 16 if they wish.
> • Parents should be allowed to educate children at home if they wish.
> • Children should be able to choose which subjects they want to study at the age of 15.

3.2 **Now record your points using the table in Appendix 2. Remember you are recording what you think the views of those directly involved might be, not your own views.**

3.3 **In groups, discuss each of the statements from Ex 3.1, comparing your ideas about the different views of the people involved.**

a) Compare what you wrote in the *different perspectives* columns for Statement 1. Use some of the *Useful language* expressions from Ex 2.2.

b) When you have completed a), give your own opinion on the first statement. What do *you* think should happen?

c) In groups, compare your answers to b). Are you able to agree?

d) Now repeat steps a–c for the other statements.

Task 4: Summarizing the outcome of a discussion

Class skill: In classes, you may have to summarize the final outcome of a long discussion. Did people agree or disagree on the main issues, and why? What were the main points for and against? You looked at this in Unit 1, Ex 2.5 (reporting back). Task 4 provides further practice in this skill.

4.1 **⊙ 6 Listen to a student summarizing a group discussion of the statement from Ex 2.1 relating to the exclusion of disruptive children. Did the group agree or disagree with the statement?**

4.2 **Look at an excerpt of the student's talk on page 24, paying attention to how the speaker organizes their points.**

The missing phrases in the blanks are where the speaker:
• states whether or not the group agreed;
• acknowledges a strong argument against their final position;
• qualifies their final position.

🎧 6 **Listen again and complete the blanks.**

> This is a difficult question, but _____ such a child
> should be excluded from school, because this would be in the best interests of most people
> concerned. _____ this action might cause some damage to the
> child's long-term ability to socialize effectively with other children, so we also agreed that
> _____ there is no other solution,
> I mean, if all else fails.

4.3 Underline the words you think are stressed in the three phrases in Task 4.2. If
necessary, listen again.

4.4 Next to each phrase in the following *Useful language* box there is a number.
This number tells you how many words are stressed when this sentence is spoken
aloud and with the correct emphasis.

a) Predict which of the words are stressed.

b) 🎧 7 Listen to a student using some of the phrases.

c) Practice saying the phrases in a natural way. Make sure you are using the correct stress.

> **Useful language:** Summarizing a discussion
>
> **Summing up your position**
>
> *We finally all agreed that …* ❸
> *After much consideration, we decided that …* ❸
> *All things considered, we felt that …* ❹
> *On balance, we felt that …* ❷
> *We couldn't reach agreement on this issue …* ❸
> *Some of us felt that …, while others …* ❹
>
> **Recognizing strong arguments against your position**
>
> *It's true that …* ❶
> *We recognized that …* ❶
> *We're fully aware that …* ❷
> *We have to acknowledge that …* ❷
>
> **Qualifying your position**
>
> *This action should only be taken if …* ❹
> *So, although we agreed with the statement, we stressed that …* ❺

4.5 Take turns to present a summary of your discussion of one of the statements from
Ex 3.1 to the class. Use the *Useful language* expressions in your summary.

After you have listened to the summaries given by the other groups, be prepared to
make comments or ask questions about what they have said.

Task 5: Online learning

It is often better to appoint a chairperson in a group discussion. This will help the management of the discussion. Task 5 looks at the role of the chairperson.

5.1 **Online learning is rapidly becoming more popular as an increasing number of students choose to study in this way. Make notes on the advantages and disadvantages of online learning in the table below.**

a) Use ideas from your own experience.

b) Read the texts on pages 75–77 about online learning. Think about whether the texts have changed your opinions and amend your notes as appropriate.

Advantages	Disadvantages
	– not all people have access to the technology

5.2 **Take part in a group discussion on the following topic.**

Online learning will eventually replace many forms of face-to-face teaching.

Think about the points you want to make and what your overall opinion of the issue is.

Appoint one group member as the chairperson to manage the discussion. The chairperson will ensure that the discussion runs smoothly and will sum up at the end. The role of the chairperson is to keep the discussion going, not to control or dominate it. A chairperson's responsibilities are listed in the box below. The appointed chairperson should refer to the *Useful language* expressions on page 26.

Note: Each person should try to make at least one contribution to the discussion. You do not need to wait for the chairperson to invite you to speak. Remember the characteristics of a good class participant from Ex 1.1. You will have 10–15 minutes for this discussion.

> **The role of chairperson includes the following responsibilities:**
>
> - getting the discussion started;
> - giving a brief overview of the topic (introducing it);
> - possibly giving definitions;
> - keeping the discussion going by encouraging everyone to participate;
> - clarifying what people say, if necessary;
> - ensuring that one person does not dominate;
> - making sure that all contributions were understood;
> - managing the time;
> - summing up the discussion at the end.

> ## Useful language: Chairing a discussion
>
> **Getting started**
>
> *Shall we begin?*
>
> *Today, we're looking at the following question/topic …*
>
> *Who would like to begin?*
>
> **Clarification**
>
> *So what you mean is …*
>
> *If I've understood you correctly, …*
>
> **Managing contributions**
>
> *Thanks, Pete, for your contribution …*
>
> *OK, Pete, would anyone else like to comment?*
>
> **Concluding**
>
> *So, to sum up, …*
>
> *We're running out of time, so …*
>
> *Does anyone want to make a final point?*
>
> *Have I forgotten anything?*

5.3 Complete the discussion review form in Appendix 9b for your group's discussion in Ex 5.2.

Study tip

To make progress with your speaking, you need to reflect on your performance in speaking activities. This will help you identify areas for improvement.

5.4 With a student from another group, compare and discuss your discussion review forms. If you were a chairperson in the discussion, join with another chairperson.

5.5 Make another entry in your student's diary.

Student's diary

Reflect on the characteristics of a good/poor discussion participant given at the start of this unit.

● Do you feel that you were a "good participant" in the discussion activities in this unit? Can you say why or why not?

● What areas do you think you need to improve on to become a better participant?

If you want, you can make a recording of your thoughts and give it to your instructor to listen to.

Unit summary

In this unit you have looked at the speaking skills you need to participate in and summarize discussions and classes. You have also looked at the role of the chairperson.

1   **Read the opinion below and discuss the questions with a partner.**

> I believe we should be allowed to leave school at the age of fifteen.

a)   Do you agree with this teenager's perspective? Why? Why not?

b)   How could you complete the sentence below?

From the point of view of an employer, …

c)   What other perspectives could this issue be considered from?

d)   Why is it important for a class participant to be able to anticipate and understand different perspectives in advance when preparing for a discussion?

2   **Complete the text below with these words and phrases from Unit 2. There is one word which you will not need to use.**

clarify	participate	dominate	overview	sum up
contribution	conclusion	time	dominate	

The role of the chairperson

In a class, the chairperson is responsible for keeping the discussion going but should not control or _____ it. They normally get the discussion started by giving a brief _____ of the topic and clarifying key concepts. They then help the discussion run smoothly by encouraging everyone to _____. This means ensuring that one person does not _____ and inviting quieter people to speak where necessary so that everyone makes at least one _____. They may also ask people to _____ any points that are unclear. The chairperson also manages the _____ and should _____ the main points at the end.

For web resources relevant to this unit, see:
www.englishforacademicstudy.com/us/student/speaking/links

These weblinks will provide you with useful information on how to participate in classes, as well as help in developing your thinking skills and discussion techniques.

3 Examining Underlying Assumptions
Changing roles in the family

In this unit you will:
- develop awareness of how to help your audience follow a presentation;
- present an article to the class, using the language of presentations;
- consider the importance of anticipating arguments before a discussion;
- practise presenting opinions and counter-arguments in a discussion.

You may find that other students from different backgrounds have completely different assumptions from you about the world, society, or what is natural. Your assumptions may be challenged. This is an opportunity to encounter different world views and perhaps to question your own underlying assumptions about society. The process of questioning and self-questioning is an important part of academic study and development.

Task 1: The meaning of *family*

1.1 **Consider one word that may mean different things to different people: *family*.**
What are your responses to the following questions?

a) What is a typical family for you?

b) In a family, what should the mother provide?

c) In a family, what should the father provide?

d) The ideal age to start a family is …

e) What does the word *family* mean to you, e.g., security, conflict?

1.2 **In groups, discuss your answers from Ex 1.1.**

Task 2: Aspects of family life

2.1 **Answer the following questions about your country.**

a) What is the average age for people to get married?

b) Is divorce common?

c) If a couple gets divorced, which parent do the children usually stay with?

d) Is it common for people to live alone?

e) What is the average age for a woman to have her first child?

f) What is the average size of a nuclear family?

g) Are many children born outside of marriage?

h) Are one-parent families common?

i) Do many people adopt children?

j) How do parents discipline their children?

k) Do parents put their children in nurseries or leave them with childminders?

2.2 **In groups, discuss the following points with reference to the questions in Ex 2.1.**

   a) What are the social norms in your country and why?

   b) Do you think the social norms are changing?

   c) If the social norms are changing, what do you think has driven these changes?

Task 3: Presenting an article (1)

Presentation skill: When you give a presentation, you need to take your audience into account and make it easy for them to follow your talk. Tasks 3 and 4 help you do this by looking at different presentation mini-skills. You will practice these skills later by presenting key ideas from an article.

3.1 **Read the text on page 78 entitled *New 'Daditude': Today's fathers are hands-on*.**

3.2 **Look at the two presentation slides in Appendix 3. Only one of the slides is a useful visual aid to support an oral summary of the article.**

   a) Decide which slide is a useful visual aid, and which is not. Give reasons.

   b) In groups, make a list of the characteristics of what makes a good visual aid.

3.3 **🎧 8 Listen to a student presenting key points from the same article.**
As you listen, refer to slide 2. Notice how the presenter expands on the points on the slide.

> **Study tip**
>
> When referring to a text, it is important to separate your own views from the writer's and to indicate clearly to the audience when you give your own views.

3.4 **Look at the extracts below and on page 30 from the presentation in Ex 3.3. In which extract does the presenter give his own views on the information in the text?**

Extract 1

"The article also gives statistics from a magazine survey of 2,000 couples. As you can see, only one-third of those asked, 34 per cent in fact, wanted to continue working full-time after having children. The majority either wanted to return to part-time work or become full-time househusbands."

Extract 2

"The article then goes on to say that the social stigma attached to men stopping work to bring up a family is disappearing … social stigma—this means something people might be ashamed of doing, that society would not approve of. As I said, this is disappearing, so you now see more men coming to schools and playgroups to pick up their children."

Extract 3

"So, the article reports on some interesting changes in social attitudes to work and fatherhood in the UK. However, it doesn't mention the effect of socioeconomic background on men's decisions or wishes regarding work and parenthood. I mean, the men who are choosing or wanting to give up work to become househusbands, are these men from high, middle, or lower income groups?"

Presentation skill: When you give your own presentations, make sure you slow down for key pieces of information so that your audience has time to understand what you are saying. It is also essential that your audience understand the key words of your presentation. It is a good idea to ensure these are on your OHT or slide and are appropriately stressed/defined in your presentation.

3.5 **Think about how presenters vary the way they speak in order to clarify information when giving a presentation.**

a) 🎧 9 Listen to the three extracts and underline where the speaker:

- slows down;
- stresses particular words or phrases.

b) Discuss why you think the speaker does this.

3.6 **Look at the transcripts on pages 99–100 for Ex 3.3 and 3.5. Find and underline eight phrases the presenter uses to refer directly to the text. Write the phrases in the *Useful language* box below.**

Example:

As the title suggests, <u>this article deals with</u> an apparent change in the role men would like to play in family life.

Useful language: Referring to an article

1 *this article deals with* …

3.7 **Discuss whether you think this article applies to men in the US.**

Task 4: Presenting an article (2)

Summarizing the main points in a presentation can be quite challenging. Sometimes it is hard to know what to omit. Imagine you are telling your friend about a film you saw. You do not tell all the details, only the main points. Similarly, when summarizing an article, the most important thing is to identify the key information.

4.1 **Read the text your instructor recommends. Make a list of four or five main points which you think are important to understanding the text.**

Make sure that you fully understand the text. If you do not understand it after checking the words or using a dictionary, check with one of your classmates—sharing ideas can often lead to a better understanding. You should not try to summarize a text if you do not understand it. When you have finished, think about the content in relation to both the US (UK) and your own country.

4.2 **With a partner or in small groups, you will prepare and present a summary of the main points of the text to the class.**

You can either choose one person to give the presentation, or divide up the presentation within your group. You have five minutes to present, with two minutes for questions. Read the list of presentation skills below before preparing your presentation.
Note: You may wish to relate to your experience in the US.

Presentation skills: There are some key points to remember when presenting information from a text.

● Read the text and identify the main ideas and/or key statistics. (If your text has a lot of facts and statistics, you need to select the ones you think are significant.)

● Identify your topic clearly in your opening and give an overview of the text.

● Carefully select what to put on your visual aid. (Do not write out sections of the text.)

● Try to express the ideas and information in your own words. (Do not read out or memorize and repeat sections of the text.)

● Distinguish between the information and ideas given in the text and your own views.

● Check the pronunciation of key words, especially those you use most frequently.

● Explain the meaning of difficult or technical words. (Note: if you have to check the meaning of a word, then your audience may not understand it either.)

● Pause and give the audience time to understand complex information.

4.3 **In groups, practice your presentation. Remember the key points from Ex 4.2.**
After your group's presenter has finished speaking, you should give some feedback, e.g.:
"You need to slow down and pause at that point. The information is complex."
"You should explain the meaning of that word."

4.4 **Present your summary of the text to the class.**

a) As you listen to each presentation, one person in each group completes the presentation assessment form in Appendix 9c. The comments you write are very important, as they will help the speaker the next time they do a presentation.

b) In your groups, discuss the following points after each presentation:

- Have you all understood the main points?

- Are there any points you were unsure of?

- Are there any questions or comments you would like to put to the presenters?

Be prepared to ask the presenters to clarify or repeat something you did not understand.

Study tip

Reflecting on your own presentation and giving feedback to other presenters can help you develop and improve your presentation skills.

4.5 **After you have listened to all the presentations, decide which was the most interesting text. Give each presenter his/her completed assessment form.**

Task 5: Arguments and counter-arguments

5.1 **Look at the following statement.**

> Women are naturally more suited to childcare than men.

You will discuss this statement in groups of four. Two of you will support this view. The other two will oppose this view.

Read the article on page 88, entitled _Cradle of civilization_. With a partner, prepare your arguments.

- What will your main points be?

- What do you think the other pair's main points will be?

- How will you counter their arguments?

Class skill: When preparing for a class or discussion, it is important to consider issues from opposing sides. This will help you to clarify your thinking and formulate your opinions on a topic. Considering an opposing position to your own can help you to strengthen your own position. On the other hand, you may find that you start to qualify or modify, or even change your own position.

5.2 **Debate the statement in Ex 5.1 in groups of four.**

a) The pair who support the statement should begin by presenting their main points.

b) The opposing pair should then counter these points and present their own points.

5.3 **Reflect on your participation in the discussion.**

- Did you state your opinion clearly?

- Did you anticipate the arguments of the other pair and counter them?

5.4 🎧 10 Listen to some students exchanging opinions on different topics. Look at the expressions below which the speakers use to exchange opinions. Check (✓) the expressions you hear.

> **Useful language:** Exchanging opinions
>
> **Asking for opinions**
>
> ☐ *What are your views on this issue?* ☐ *Do you agree?*
>
> **Presenting your own opinion**
>
> ☐ *Well, I think …* ☐ *It seems to me that …*
>
> ☐ *In my view, …*
>
> **Countering the other person's opinion**
>
> ☐ *I take your point, but …* ☐ *I understand what you're saying, but …*
>
> ☐ *Well, I'm not sure if that's quite true …* ☐ *But surely …*

5.5 Change partners and prepare to discuss one of the following statements. Decide which pair will support the view given and which pair will oppose it.

It is better to wait until you are older to start a family.

Living on your own has more advantages than disadvantages.

Wealth will not bring you happiness.

Prepare for your discussion as in Ex 5.1. Use some of the *Useful language* expressions in Ex 5.4.

Student's diary

Do you feel more confident presenting in front of an audience?

● How did this unit help you?

● What do you feel you still need to do to improve your presentation skills?

Do you feel more confident participating in discussions?

● How did this unit help you?

● What do you feel you still need to do to be a better participant in class discussions?

Presentation skill: If you want further guidelines on developing your presentation skills, see Appendix 4.

Unit Summary

In this unit you have looked at how to present articles and practiced clarifying opinions and expressing counter-arguments in academic situations.

1 Think about the question below. Then complete the slides below using the words and phrases in the box. There is one word which you will not need to use.

How can you make sure important information is clear in a presentation?

stress	headings	information	slide	key words	bullet points	highlight

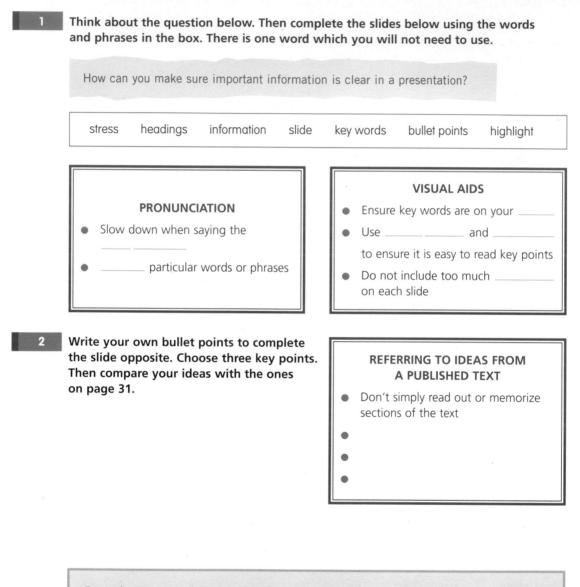

PRONUNCIATION

● Slow down when saying the _____

● _____ particular words or phrases

VISUAL AIDS

● Ensure key words are on your _____

● Use _____ _____ and _____ to ensure it is easy to read key points

● Do not include too much _____ on each slide

2 Write your own bullet points to complete the slide opposite. Choose three key points. Then compare your ideas with the ones on page 31.

REFERRING TO IDEAS FROM A PUBLISHED TEXT

● Don't simply read out or memorize sections of the text

●

●

●

For web resources relevant to this unit, see:
www.englishforacademicstudy.com/us/student/speaking/links

These weblinks will provide you with further information on how to conduct presentations, as well as additional information about attitudes towards the family.

4 Reading into Speaking
A healthy lifestyle

In this unit you will:
- use a text to support or modify your ideas;
- practice active listening;
- develop strategies to check your understanding as a listener;
- exchange information effectively by anticipating your listener's difficulties.

When preparing for a class, you will often need to refer to reading texts on the topic in order to develop your ideas further. You will probably have your own ideas on the topic before you start reading. As you read, you may find support for your ideas. However, you may find that you change or adjust your views as you read. This may in turn influence the ideas you present in the class. The ability to integrate and develop ideas from your reading is an essential part of academic life.

Task 1: Questionnaire

Complete the following questionnaire about yourself.

How healthy is your lifestyle?

a) How often do you exercise?

b) How many hours a day do you spend sitting?

c) How regular are your meals?

d) How often do you eat fruit and vegetables?

e) Do you prepare your own food or do you eat processed food?

f) How often do you eat junk food?

g) Do you take vitamin supplements?

h) How many times a year do you have a cold?

i) Are you a smoker?

With a partner, use the questionnaire to interview each other. Do you think your partner has a healthy lifestyle?

Task 2: Who is responsible?

Nowadays there is often discussion about who is responsible for various aspects of life. Is it the individual or the government? For example, recently the governments in many countries have introduced a ban on smoking in all public places. In other countries, individuals can still decide whether or not they wish to smoke in a public place. What is the situation in your country?

2.1 **You are going to compare two ideas. Read the following statements. Do you agree or disagree with each one? Give reasons for your answers. Then, discuss each statement in groups.**

> It is the responsibility of the individual to give up smoking.

> It is the responsibility of employers to reduce stress levels among their staff.

2.2 **Who else might be responsible for the issues mentioned in Ex 2.1?**

Class skill: You need to spend time preparing for a class. What do you think about the topic? Does any of the reading you do influence what you think? How will you express what you want to say? Task 3 asks you to prepare for a discussion.

Task 3: Preparation for a class discussion

You are now going to look at how information from a text can help develop your ideas. You will then practice discussing your opinion with reference to the ideas from the text.

3.1 **Read the following statement. With a partner, discuss whether you agree with this statement. Give reasons for your opinions.**

> It is the responsibility of individuals themselves to avoid becoming obese by ensuring they have a balanced diet and a healthy lifestyle.

Source: Crown copyright 2007

When you have finished, write down your opinion in the middle of a blank piece of paper (maximum three lines).

3.2 **Read the text on page 90 about government attitudes to health in the US and answer the questions below.**

a) Is there anything in the text which supports the opinions you expressed in Ex 3.1?

b) Is there anything in the text which might make you modify or change your opinions?

c) Does the text provide you with additional ideas?

3.3 Write relevant points from Ex 3.2 around your original opinion on your piece of paper from Ex 3.1. Add points which develop, change, or support your view.

Example:

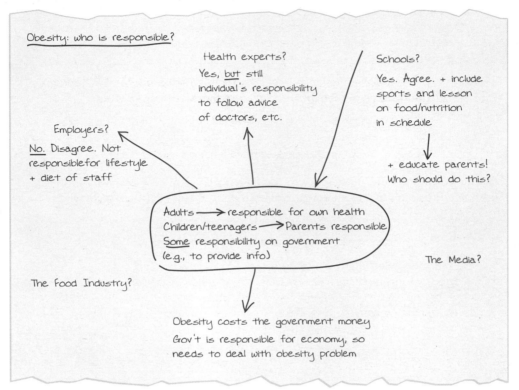

Obesity: who is responsible?

Health experts?
Yes, but still individual's responsibility to follow advice of doctors, etc.

Schools?
Yes. Agree. + include sports and lesson on food/nutrition in schedule

Employers?
No. Disagree. Not responsible for lifestyle + diet of staff

+ educate parents!
Who should do this?

Adults → responsible for own health
Children/teenagers → Parents responsible
Some responsibility on government (e.g., to provide info)

The Media?

The Food Industry?

Obesity costs the government money
Gov't is responsible for economy, so needs to deal with obesity problem

3.4 You are going to discuss the statement from Ex 3.1 in groups of four or five.

a) Prepare what you are going to say. You may refer to your notes and the text, if you wish.

b) Now discuss the statement in groups.

3.5 Summarize the outcome of your discussion for the class. Did your group agree or disagree with the statement overall?

Study tip

You can prepare for a class by deciding on your opinion and then reading and noting down points that confirm, develop, or challenge it. This makes it easier to clarify and summarize your ideas and those you have read.

Class skill: Discussions are interactive. You do not just present your own views, you listen and react to what other people are saying. Task 4 looks at this aspect of classes. After you have looked at and practiced appropriate language expressions, Ex 4.4 requires you to put these skills and language into practice in a class situation.

Speaking & Pronunciation

Task 4: Being an active listener

Listening is also an important aspect of participating in a discussion. You need to listen because your ideas may be influenced by what other students say. An important aspect of listening actively is making sure that you have understood correctly and showing when you do not understand. As a speaker, you also need to make sure that people have understood you.

4.1 **Consider your role as a listener and speaker in the discussion you had in Task 3. Think about the following questions, and discuss these with your group.**

a) As a listener, did you interrupt the speaker if you did not understand something?

b) As a speaker, did you make sure that your listeners were following you?

4.2 **Look at the expressions in the *Useful language* box.**
🎧 11 **Listen to some of these expressions in context. Check (✓) the ones that you hear.**

> ## Useful language: Clarifying and confirming understanding
>
> **Confirming understanding as a listener**
>
> ☐ *So what you're saying is …*
>
> ☐ *So in your view, …*
>
> ☐ *If I understand you correctly, you're saying …*
>
> **Checking understanding as a speaker**
>
> ☐ *Do you understand what I mean?*
>
> ☐ *Do you follow what I am saying?*
>
> ☐ *Am I making sense?*
>
> **Showing that you do not understand**
>
> ☐ *I'm not sure I understand what you mean.*
>
> ☐ *I didn't quite follow you. Could you explain that point again, please?*
>
> ☐ *Could you repeat that, please?*

4.3 **With a partner, look at the following statements and follow the instructions on the next page.**

Statement 1

> Free health care should not be given to smokers.

Statement 2

> Advertising of junk food should be banned.

Student A: Decide whether you agree or disagree with the first statement and give the main reasons for your opinion to Student B. Make sure that he or she understands your points, using one or more expressions from the *Useful language* box in Ex 4.2.

Student B: Listen and confirm your understanding of Student A's opinion by summarizing what he or she says. Use at least one of the phrases for confirming understanding from the box in Ex 4.2.

Now change roles and discuss the second statement.

4.4 **You will now practice the discussion from Task 3 again, but using the interactive strategies from Ex 4.3.**

  a) Review the points you wrote down on obesity from Task 3.

  b) Form a new group with different people.

  c) Discuss the statement from Ex 3.1. This time, make sure you include the strategies and *Useful language* that you have just practiced.

4.5 **Complete the discussion review form in Appendix 9d. In groups, discuss your answers.**

Task 5: Comparing information

Relating information from a text to someone who has not read it is an aspect of academic life. You need to inform your listener and make sure they have understood the main points. It is unhelpful to exchange information without checking understanding. This section deals with exchanging information in a cooperative way.

5.1 **Answer the following questions on the topic of stress.**

  a) What are the main causes of stress?

  b) How does stress affect your health?

  c) Can stress ever be good for you?

  d) What are some ways of dealing with stress?

Discuss your answers with a partner.

5.2 **Your instructor will give you one of two texts on the topic of stress so that you can then exchange information about the texts in pairs.**

As you read:

  ● ensure that you fully understand the information;

  ● anticipate what difficulties your listener will have;

  ● use some of the strategies from Task 4.

5.3 **Complete the appropriate column in the table on page 40 with information from your text. Check your answers with people who have read the same text as you.**

Speaking & Pronunciation

5.4 **Exchanging information: Work with a partner who read the other text and follow the steps below.**

a) Explain the information you wrote in the table to your partner. Use your notes from the column you filled in—do not look at the original text.

b) Listen to your partner's explanation of the other text and complete the other section of the table.

Make sure you and your partner fully understand each other as you complete the table. This means you should:

● check the pronunciation of any difficult words before you start;

● make sure your partner has understood what you say;

● ask your partner to repeat or explain if you do not understand;

● remember to use the *Useful language* expressions from Ex 4.2 for checking understanding as a speaker and as a listener.

Study tip

Successful class participation involves checking and signaling whether you have understood other group members, and making sure that they have understood you. This involves ensuring you understand the topic before the discussion and cooperating in exchanging information during it.

	Article A: Stress: To what extent can it be controlled?	Article B: Stress: Keeping things in perspective
Definition of stress		
Examples of symptoms of stress		
Suggestions for dealing with stress		

5.5 **What similarities and differences did you find between the information given in the two texts? Discuss the differences with your partner.**

5.6 **In groups, decide what information from the texts would be useful for a discussion on the following topic.**

Relaxation techniques are the best method for dealing with stress.

Student's diary

Reflect on your participation in the discussions in this unit.

● How easy do you find it to follow discussions and make relevant contributions?

● What problems do you have with this?

● Can you think of ways to help you improve your participation?

● In discussions and presentations, how can you help people to follow what you are saying?

Unit Summary

In this unit you have practiced preparing for discussions and relating information from texts to others. You have also worked on developing your active listening skills.

1   **Think about and/or discuss your answers to the following questions.**

  a) What can you do before a class to prepare for a topic you are uncertain about?

  b) What can you do or say in a class if you are not clear what someone means?

  c) What can you do or say in a class if you are uncertain whether or not you understand someone else's explanation of something?

  d) How can you make sure that someone else has understood what you said?

2   **Read the extract from a discussion about health below. Fill the blanks with suitable phrases for clarifying and confirming understanding.**

> A: I think people worry too much about their diet. The government keeps saying our society is overweight because we eat the wrong things, but I don't think it's true.
>
> B: So, what you're _____ is that obesity is not an important issue?
>
> A: Well, I agree that a lot of people are overweight, but it may be due to other factors. Am I _____ _____ ? People used to have very active lives and they had to keep warm, so they ate a lot but still kept thin.
>
> B: I don't quite _____ _____. Could _____ _____ _____ _____ a little more clearly?
>
> A: I mean that people are putting on weight because they have a modern lifestyle. Do you _____ _____ __ _____ ?
>
> B: If I _____ _____ correctly, you think we are overweight because of our lifestyle and that it's an inevitable part of modern life.

3   **Look at the *Useful language* box on page 38 and compare the phrases in the blanks above with the ones you used in Ex 2.**

> For web resources relevant to this unit, see:
> **www.englishforacademicstudy.com/us/student/speaking/links**
>
> These weblinks will provide you with interesting information on health-based topics.

5 The Use of Data
The influence of the media

In this unit you will:
- practice describing charts and data;
- practice seminar skills by building on what previous speakers have said;
- identify and practise using phrases to refer to other speakers.

Data is a key part of academic study. Charts, graphs and tables are often included in both written work and presentations. They are used as evidence, to support the points the writer or speaker is trying to make.

Task 1: Matching definitions

1.1 **Match the words for TV and radio programs with their definitions.**

a) soap opera ☐

b) quiz show ☐

c) reality TV ☐

d) chat show ☐

e) sitcom ☐

f) documentary ☐

g) phone-in ☐

h) classic drama ☐

i) makeover program ☐

j) game show ☐

k) mini-series ☐

1 A program in which the public takes part by phoning in with comments.

2 A long-running drama of the day-to-day experiences of a community of characters.

3 A program in which contestants try to score points by answering questions correctly.

4 An informative, in-depth examination of a fairly serious topic.

5 A program in which contestants take part in various games to win prizes.

6 An adaptation of a major work of literature.

7 A program in which a presenter asks a celebrity to talk about him/herself.

8 A team of experts redecorate your house, redesign your garden, or change your image.

9 A program in which a group of people (usually from the public) are filmed over a period of time.

10 A comedy of character and situation involving the same characters in each episode.

11 A program which has several episodes with the same characters.

Task 2: Discussion: TV programs

2.1 **Discuss your opinions in groups.**

a) Which kind of program is most popular in your country?

b) What kind of audience do the programs in Ex 1.1 appeal to?

c) Why are reality TV programs so popular?

d) Which kind of program do you watch most often in your own country?

e) Which kind of program do you least enjoy?

f) Which kinds of program have you seen on English-language television, if any?

2.2 **Think of a particular program (in your country or the country where you are studying) that you especially enjoyed or disliked. Briefly describe the program and explain your reaction to it.**

Presentation skill: When giving a presentation, you may need to refer to charts and graphs to support your point. It is important to guide your audience to the main points of the data or those points which are relevant to the argument you are presenting. You will practice doing this in Task 3.

Task 3: Presenting information

3.1 **Look at the graph. It shows the results of a survey of the changing patterns of people going to the movies, according to age. What trends does it show? Discuss with a partner.**

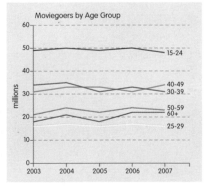

3.2 **⊙ 12 Listen to the description of the data shown and answer the following questions.**

a) What details does the speaker highlight?

b) What point is the speaker making by showing this data?

3.3 **⊙ 12 Listen to the recording again and fill in the blanks in the excerpt.**

_____ movie admissions per age group between 2003 and 2007. _____, young people aged between 15 and 24 are the most likely age group to go to the movies. There were 48 million admissions from this age group in the US in 2007. In 2007, there were 34 million admissions from the next most frequent age group, _____. The overall admissions across all age groups have risen slightly. _____ going to the movies is still a popular form of entertainment, despite the arrival of videos, DVDs, and computer games.

Source: Motion Picture Association of America, Movie Attendance Study, 2007, http://www.mpaa.org/MovieAttendanceStudy.pdf.

3.4 For your next class, find a chart or graph which presents information which interests you. Follow the steps below.

a) Select the information that the graph shows that you would like to present to the class.

b) Prepare the point(s) you want to make. Be prepared to use the chart to support your point(s).

c) Give your presentation. Make sure you use some of the *Useful language* expressions below in your presentation.

Presentation skill: When you present data, you should start by briefly outlining what the data is about. You should then comment on the features that are relevant and support the points you are making.

> **Useful language:** Referring to data
>
> *This graph gives information about …*
>
> *This line here shows …*
>
> *This chart describes …*
>
> *As these figures illustrate, …*
>
> *This chart clearly shows that …*

Task 4: Listening

4.1 🎧 13 **You are going to hear a journalist talking about the British Broadcasting Corporation (BBC). Read the questions below before you listen. Then answer them as you listen.**

a) What were the three purposes of the BBC when it was originally set up?

b) In what ways did John Reith, the first director general of the BBC, believe that the BBC should be independent?

c) In the 1920s, what caused conflict between the BBC and the government?

d) More recently, what was the main area of conflict between the government and the BBC?

e) How does the BBC finance itself?

4.2 **Read the transcript on pages 102–104 to check your answers.**

4.3 **The journalist comments that "the BBC is still the most trusted organization in the country." To what extent do you think that television coverage of news events can be trusted in the US?**

Task 5: Building on what the previous speaker has said

In Unit 4, you looked at the skill of active listening. This is important because your contributions to the discussion need to relate to what has been said previously. You may need to show this by referring to previous speakers. This helps the discussion to develop a sense of direction.

In addition, you may find that your ideas develop and change as you interact with other students. You might have a clearer idea of what you think or what your position is by the end of a class. Task 5 looks at this aspect of classes.

5.1 **Discuss the following questions with a partner.**

a) What does *freedom of speech* mean to you?

b) Are there any negative aspects of freedom of speech?

5.2 **Look at the following statements. Decide if you agree or disagree with each one, and why.**

a) Freedom of speech is absolutely necessary in a democracy.

b) There should be no limits on freedom of speech.

c) Complete freedom of speech may mean that some individuals may feel unsafe in a society.

d) The government needs to limit freedom of speech to protect minority groups.

5.3 🎧 14 **Listen to three students discussing freedom of speech and answer the following questions.**

a) The two women state that there should be no limit on freedom of speech. What does the man believe?

b) What are his reasons?

c) Does he change his opinion?

5.4 **Look at the transcript on pages 104–105. Underline the phrases which the speakers use to refer to the comments of other speakers.**

Example:

When you say "an absolute principle", do you mean that anyone can say or broadcast or print anything they want …

5.5 **Write the phrases in the *Useful language* box below.**

> **Useful language:** Referring to other speakers
>
> _____   _____
>
> _____   _____
>
> _____   _____
>
> _____   _____

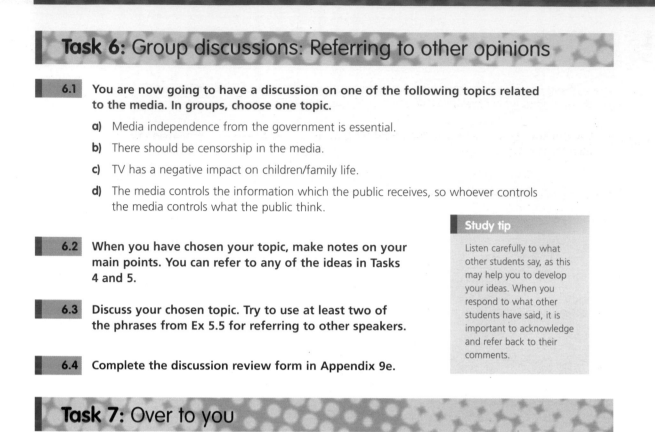

Task 6: Group discussions: Referring to other opinions

6.1 You are now going to have a discussion on one of the following topics related to the media. In groups, choose one topic.

a) Media independence from the government is essential.

b) There should be censorship in the media.

c) TV has a negative impact on children/family life.

d) The media controls the information which the public receives, so whoever controls the media controls what the public think.

6.2 When you have chosen your topic, make notes on your main points. You can refer to any of the ideas in Tasks 4 and 5.

6.3 Discuss your chosen topic. Try to use at least two of the phrases from Ex 5.5 for referring to other speakers.

6.4 Complete the discussion review form in Appendix 9e.

Task 7: Over to you

7.1 For the next session, find a recent article from an English-language media source that reports on the news or events in your country. Then answer the questions below about what you have read.

Choose your article from a newspaper or magazine or from the web. A good approach is to go to the website of a newspaper such as www.nytimes.com or broadcaster such as www.npr.org and do an Archive Search.

a) *What* events or issues does the article report on? Summarize the main points. (See the *Useful language* box in Unit 3, Ex 3.6.)

b) *How* does the article report on the events? Do you think there is any bias in the reporting, or does it seem to be objective? Do you think it might mislead readers in any way about your country? Do you think this information was reported in a similar way in the media in your own country?

7.2 Bring a copy of the article to the next session. Be prepared to report back on points a) and b). You will have two minutes.

Student's diary

● On your future courses, what sort of data do you anticipate you will be dealing with?

● Do you feel more confident in describing data orally? If not, what do you feel you need to practice more?

● Has your participation in group discussion changed since the beginning of the course? How?

● What aspects of participation in group discussion do you still find difficult?

Unit Summary

In this unit you have practiced describing graphs and data. You have also practiced using different ways of referring to other speakers or articles and building on what they have said.

1 **Look at the table below about movie-going in the UK and discuss the answers to questions a–c.**

British movie-going—19-year trends												
Age	1984	1987	1990	1993	1996	1997	1998	1999	2000	2001	2002	2003
7+	38%	58%	64%	69%	72%	75%	83%	78%	86%	82%	82%	83%
7-14	73%	88%	85%	93%	95%	95%	97%	95.5%	97%	97%	98%	91%
15-34	55%	74%	83%	86%	90%	94%	96%	93%	95%	94%	94%	87%
35+	21%	42%	49%	53.5%	58%	60%	74%	66%	79%	73%	74%	60%

a) What does the table show?

b) Find the trends in this chart that support the following claim: *going to the movies became more popular amongst younger people in the UK in the 1990s.*

c) What other trends in this chart are significant?

d) Write a paragraph to describe the data. Use some of the words in the box below in your paragraph.

describe   illustrate   rise   figures   increase   highest percentage   clearly   noticeably

e) Compare your paragraph with the one on page 43 and make sure that you used the *Useful language* correctly.

2 **The sentences below refer to points that other people have made in a discussion or published article. Correct the mistake in each one.**

a) Can I pick on John's point about limiting freedom of speech?

b) Ahmed talked about democratic ideals. Following off from that point, I'd like to talk about the situation in the US.

c) This article does some fair arguments, but it doesn't go far enough.

d) The article makes interesting point about freedom of speech and responsibility.

For web resources relevant to this unit, see:
www.englishforacademicstudy.com/us/student/speaking/links

These weblinks will provide you with further help on dealing with charts and data.

6 Consolidation Unit

In the past five units, you have worked on the following skills:
- presenting your point of view and looking at different perspectives;
- presenting, agreeing with and countering an argument;
- building on what previous speakers have said;
- taking the role of chairperson;
- using appropriate language phrases.

Class skills practice

In this consolidation unit, you will have the opportunity to practice further the skills you have learned by leading a class discussion. This will involve being responsible for the initial input in the class as well as summing up at the end. This is different from chairing a discussion, where you are only responsible for ensuring the discussion goes smoothly.

Although you should all prepare for the class, your opportunity to actually conduct a class will depend on the time available.

Task 1: Initial preparation for the class

1.1 Select a topic for your class discussion.
Choose a controversial subject. It needs to be one that is of interest to the others in your class and one they will be able to discuss. For ideas on discussion topics, see Appendix 5.

1.2 Prepare an overview of the topic.
This should be a summary of the main issues, as well as a list of discussion points for the group to consider. Alternatively, you might like to present points on both sides of the issue before opening it up to discussion by all the participants.

1.3 In groups, discuss the following advice for the class leader. Can you think of any further points to add?

- You will have 20 minutes for the class, including: presenting the topic (max. four minutes), discussion, and summing up the discussion at the end.

- Ensure that everyone has the opportunity to participate in the discussion.

- In order to keep the discussion going if there is silence, you will need to: build on what has been said before, ask a question, or invite a specific person to contribute.

Task 2: Model demonstration

2.1 Discuss with another student the characteristics of a good class participant.
You can refer to Unit 2 if you need to refresh your memory.

2.2 Your instructor will demonstrate how to lead a class discussion. During the demonstration, complete the assessment form in Appendix 9f.

2.3 **Give feedback on the class leader (your instructor) using the assessment form as a basis for your comments.**

During this feedback you will learn how to make your comments effectively.

Task 3: Presentation skills

3.1 **Discuss the following presentation skills you have worked on during this course with your partner and think about how you would use these in a class.**

- Planning a presentation

- Selecting and organizing your ideas

- Introducing a topic

- Delivering a presentation clearly

- Using visual aids

- Using signpost expressions to guide the listener

3.2 **Review the *Useful language* boxes from each unit and think about how you could use the language in an appropriate way.**

Task 4: Leading the class

These will take place at a time to be arranged by your instructor. The allocated class leader will run the class and the rest of the students will participate. Use the assessment form in Appendix 9f to give feedback to each class leader.

Student's diary

After you have led a class, reflect on the experience in your diary.

- How did you feel immediately afterwards?

- What aspects did you feel satisfied with?

- What aspects of managing a class do you feel you still need to work on?

For web resources relevant to this unit, see:
www.englishforacademicstudy.com/us/student/speaking/links

These weblinks will provide you with further help on how to give a presentation.

Speaking & Pronunciation

7 Supporting Your Point of View
The world of work

In this unit you will:
- prepare for a discussion by thinking through the issues beforehand;
- use a listening source to support your viewpoint;
- consider strategies for entering into a discussion;
- research and plan a presentation.

In academic study, you will often have to refer to a variety of written and spoken resources. In a class, you can use these to give evidence to support your viewpoint, whether or not you agree with the viewpoint expressed in an article. However, before you consult these sources, it is useful to spend some time thinking about the topic and working out your opinion on the basis of what you already know. Your position may subsequently change as you engage with the texts and the views of other students.

Task 1: Your attitude to work

1.1 **After you graduate, you will probably be looking for work or returning to work. How important are the following aspects of work to you?**

a) Put a check (✔) in the appropriate box (5 = very important; 1 = less important).

b) Add three further aspects of work which are important to you.

c) Compare and discuss your responses with a partner.

	1	2	3	4	5
The amount I earn					
The people I work with					
The amount of responsibility I have					
The variety of tasks I do					
The degree of challenge I have					
The job security I have					
The possibilities I have of promotion					
The number of hours I work					
The possibility of working flexible hours					

1.2 Careers advice services often use questionnaires to help direct people towards a suitable career. See Appendix 6 for an example careers questionnaire.

a) Complete the questionnaire for homework. Bring the completed questionnaire to your next session when your instructor will give you the key so you can analyze the results.

b) Discuss your questionnaire results in groups. To what extent do you agree with the analysis?

Task 2: Finding a job in your country

Discuss the following questions with a partner or in groups.

a) How easy is it for graduates to find work in your country at the moment?

b) What sort of information do job applicants usually provide to employers on a curriculum vitae?

c) What is most important to employers in your country:

- the reputation of the university you attended?

- the qualification you obtained (undergraduate degree, graduate degree)?

- the result you obtained?

- the people you know?

- other factors?

Task 3: Gender at work

Look at the following and read the short extract. Then answer these questions.

a) What do you think are the most significant trends in the table?

b) How does men's pay compare with women's?

c) What other obstacles might women face in gaining senior positions?

d) How does this trend compare with the pattern in your country?

	1979	2007
Women in employment	41.2 million	67.8 million
Full-time gender pay gap	37.7%	19.8%
Working mothers with school children	54.5%	71.3%
Working mothers with pre-school children	41.1%	60.1%

Source: Women in the Labor Force: A Databook, Report 1011, US Department of Labor, U.S. Bureau of Statistics, December 2008

"... some companies are reluctant to hire or promote a woman when relocation with a spouse is involved. ... management may make the decision for the woman by eliminating her as a candidate."

Source: Women in the workplace: making progress in Corporate America, Landon S, *USA Today* 11/1/96

Task 4: Equal opportunities

You are going to discuss the following topic.

> There should be equal opportunities for men and women to do any job.

4.1 **Discuss the following questions with a partner.**

a) Are some jobs more appropriate for men than women? Give examples and say why.

b) Are some jobs more appropriate for women than men? Give examples and say why.

c) To what extent do nature or nurture influence the jobs men and women choose to do?

4.2 You are going to listen to an interview with Sonia Gurjao, the author of a UK research paper entitled *Inclusivity: the Changing Role of Women in the Construction Workforce*.

Before you listen, read the following extract from the paper's introduction.

> The UK's construction industry is facing a skills shortage that is a threat to the long-term health of the industry. It is suffering recruitment problems with its traditional source of labor—young men aged 16–19. Efforts are being made to recruit women into the workforce, but with limited success. In the short term, the industry is filling the skills gap using workers from low-wage economies. What is needed is a skilled workforce that sees its long-term future in the UK construction industry. To meet the challenge of the skills gap, the recruitment of women is no longer simply a nice thing to do; it has become a necessity.
>
> Women in the UK construction industry currently account for under ten per cent of the workforce, reflecting their under-representation in an industry that fails to attract and retain women.

Source: Gurjao, S. (2006). *Inclusivity: the Changing Role of Women in the Construction Workforce.* The CIOB.

4.3 **Read the questions that the interviewer asks Sonia.**

a) What are the reasons why more women today are participating in the labor market?

b) Is the construction industry a common career choice for women?

c) Why does the construction industry need more women to join it?

d) Has the construction industry made any attempts to recruit women into the industry?

e) The construction industry has a problem with keeping the women who join it. Why is that and is there a solution to the problem?

f) What are the main barriers women face today in joining or staying in the construction industry?

4.4 🎧 15 **Listen to the interview.**

a) Take notes of Sonia's replies to the questions.

_____

_____

_____

_____

_____

_____

b) Is there any information from the interview you might be able to use in your discussion?

4.5 **Discuss the topic in groups. You may appoint a chairperson to manage the discussion.**

Task 5: Taking your turn

During a class, it is sometimes difficult to find the "right moment" to make your point. When you want to make a point, someone else speaks first, and then the discussion moves on to a different aspect. In addition, you may find that discussions between several people are often not very "tidy," because people may respond to different points at the same time.

Task 5 looks at some examples of this situation, and also some _Useful language_ to help you take a turn in a discussion appropriately.

5.1 **Think back to the discussion in Task 4.**

a) Do any of the following statements below describe how you felt about your role in the discussion (or in discussions generally)?

You wanted to speak, but did not have the opportunity because:

- the discussion moved too quickly and you missed a chance to speak at a relevant point;

- other people wanted to speak at the same time as you;

- you did not want to interrupt or speak over other people.

b) What strategies or language do you think you could use to make your points or respond more effectively in the above situations?

5.2 **Read the _Useful language_ expressions on page 54 and decide which you could have used in the discussion in Task 4.**

Task 6: The changing nature of work in the 21st century

When you give a presentation, you need to ensure the main points are relevant to your focus. Task 6 looks at this aspect of presentations.

6.1   **Check your understanding of the following topics.**

telecommuting   ethical working practices

the 24/7 society   working flexitime

the knowledge-based economy   corporate culture

the decline in manufacturing industry

job-sharing   management style

6.2 In groups, choose one of the topics in Ex 6.1. Choose one of the following questions to discuss in relation to your chosen topic. This will help you find a focus for your presentation.

a) What are its causes and what are its consequences?

b) Is there a problem associated with it? What are possible solutions to the problem?

c) Can aspects of it be compared and contrasted, e.g., between different cultures?

d) How has it developed over time? How might it continue to develop?

Example:

Topic: Telecommuting

Question: What are its causes and what are its consequences?

Causes: —technological developments allowing easier communication between workplace and home

—more women wishing to work from home after having children

Consequences: Can you think of any consequences?

6.3 Develop your ideas into a full presentation in your groups. You should carry out some research in your group by consulting a range of sources. Decide how you will divide up the research and report back on your ideas.

Presentation skill: You should refer to your sources in your presentation, incorporating data or quotations where appropriate. These should be acknowledged.

6.4 Give your presentations to the class. Evaluate the other presentations according to the following criteria.

Organization

● Are the main ideas logically ordered?

● Are the introduction and conclusion linked to the main ideas?

Content

● Are the main ideas relevant to the focus?

● Are the ideas developed in sufficient depth?

Student's diary

● Which activity did you enjoy most in this unit?

● Have you moderated any of your views as a result of what you listened to and discussed in the unit?

● Do you prefer to give a presentation where the title is fixed, or do you prefer to choose your own title? Please give a reason for your choice.

● What aspects of giving a presentation do you still find difficult?

Unit Summary

In this unit you have continued to work on preparing for discussions and have practiced taking turns in a class. You have also prepared and given a presentation on the topic of work.

1 **Discuss what you can do or say in class scenarios like the ones below. Think of some useful phrases that you could use to interrupt or deal with the situation.**

a) Anna and Tom have been arguing a point. Jose keeps trying to say something, but is rather reluctant to interrupt.

b) Your instructor asks a question, and both you and another student start to reply at the same time.

c) You start to explain something but the discussion moves on and you cannot finish what you were saying. Later on, there is an opportunity for you to finish your explanation.

d) You feel that Anna made a very important point earlier in the class, and you would like to return to it.

2 **Think back to the discussions and/or presentations in this unit and answer the questions below.**

a) Were your ideas sufficiently researched and developed? What could you have included to make them more interesting?

b) Did you use information from talks or lectures you heard to back up your opinion? How could you do this (more) effectively?

c) Did you use statistics from tables or articles you read to back up your opinion? How could you do this (more) effectively?

d) Were your ideas ordered logically or did you leave something out? How could you improve the organization of your ideas?

For web resources relevant to this unit, see:
www.englishforacademicstudy.com/us/student/speaking/links

These weblinks will provide you with further help on how to give a presentation, as well as information on issues related to students working or studying abroad.

8

Collecting and Presenting Data
Protecting the environment

In this unit you will:
- design a questionnaire and obtain feedback on it;
- collect and present data;
- participate in a debate;
- give a presentation on a global issue.

On your academic course, you may be required to collect, analyze, and present data. You may have to design the method of data collection yourself. In this unit you are going to choose a topic, design a questionnaire, analyze the results, and then present them.

Task 1: Designing a questionnaire

1.1 **Imagine that you want to learn about people's attitudes towards the environment. Start preparing a questionnaire about some of the following issues.**

recycling in the home	saving energy in the home	use of transport
shopping for eco-friendly products		supporting environmental groups

When preparing your questionnaire, you need to:

a) decide what the overall aim of your questionnaire is. For example, your overall aim might be to determine how much responsibility people are taking individually to protect and preserve the environment.

b) decide what the focus of your questionnaire is, e.g., what people do in relation to their home;

c) identify eight to ten questions for your topic;

d) make sure each question elicits relevant information.

Study tip

When designing a questionnaire, make sure you have a clear overall aim. This will help ensure you elicit the information you require.

Think of this topic in the broadest sense, including issues such as throwing things away when they are still functional.

Sometimes, questions in questionnaires are poorly designed, because they do not elicit the information required, are not appropriate, or do not allow for the subject to give the answer which is true for them.

1.2 Look at some examples of poorly designed questions. What is wrong with each question? How could each one be improved?

1 How old are you? ———————————— [ ]

2 Do you use public transport often? ———————— [ ]

3 Do you recycle:

—every day? ———————————————— [ ]

—once a week? ——————————————— [ ]

—once a year? ——————————————— [ ]

4 Do you like environmentally friendly products? ——— [ ]

1.3 In groups of three, write eight to ten questions that would be suitable for the questionnaire discussed in Ex 1.1.

1.4 Exchange questionnaires with another group. Evaluate their questionnaire.

● Does it elicit the relevant information?

● Are any of the questions poorly designed?

● Have you any suggestions for improvement?

1.5 Choose one of the questions from your questionnaire.

a) Ask all your classmates the same question, making a note of their responses.

b) Report back on your findings to the rest of the class. Use the expressions in the *Useful language* box.

Useful language: Expressing quantity

Most			
Nearly all		of those interviewed/questioned …	reported/
Approximately	half	of the subjects …	stated/
Approaching	a third		
Just under		of the respondents …	claimed that …
Just over	50 per cent		

1.6 In groups of three, brainstorm ideas and choose a new topic for your own questionnaire. You will need to bring three copies of the questionnaire to the next session in order to pilot it with another group.

Task 2: Piloting your questionnaire

2.1 Give your questionnaire to another group to complete.

2.2 Complete the questionnaire you have received from another group. In groups, discuss the following questions and evaluate the questionnaire.

- Are the questions clear?
- Could the questionnaire be improved in any way, e.g., a more effective layout?
- Are there any other questions which could be added?

2.3 Return the questionnaire to the group which designed it, and explain any comments you have.

2.4 Revise your questionnaire in view of the feedback you received from the other group.

Task 3: Administering your questionnaire

3.1 Practice asking the questions in your questionnaire with someone from another group. Check pronunciation of individual words with your instructor if necessary.

3.2 You now need to collect data from 15 other people, using your questionnaire. Interview your subjects face-to-face and note down their answers.

Presentation skill: Data is often included in presentations, as discussed in Unit 5, to support the points you are making. If you have collected the data yourself, you need to think about how to present the data and what language to use. See the *Useful language* box on page 44 and Task 4 below.

Task 4: Reporting back on your findings

4.1 You need to decide how you are going to present your data, e.g., *pie chart, bar graph, table.*
Your choice will be determined by the kind of information you want to present—what format will allow you to present your information most effectively?

4.2 🔊 16 Listen to a student using *Useful language* expressions from Ex 1.5. Underline the words or phrases in the box that the speaker uses.

4.3 Now present your own data to a partner. Use some of the *Useful language* expressions from Ex 1.5.

Presentation skill: You should follow the steps below when presenting data that you have gathered in a questionnaire.

- Present data.
- Highlight significant data.
- Discuss the implications of the data.
- Evaluate the design of the questionnaire; how well did it work?

Task 5: Participating in a debate

A debate is a formal forum of discussion that can also help you develop your ideas and perspectives on issues. In a debate situation, there are two teams: one in favor of the motion and the other against. There are three people on each team. Two members of the team have to make a speech. The third member of each team should be ready to pick up points made by the opposition and respond. The other team members can help this member by passing on any ideas.

5.1 **You are going to debate the following motion.**

> Protection of the environment is mainly dependent on government policies; leaving it to individuals will not work.

a) Organize your teams and audience and decide who will judge the debate.

b) Decide which team will argue in favor of the motion and which team will argue against it.

5.2 **Prepare for the debate with your team.**

a) List as many points as possible to support your side, with examples and evidence.

b) Try to think of points which the opposition will raise. Come up with counter-arguments.

c) Decide which team member will make which points.

5.3 **Make sure you understand the following rules.**

- Each person has a limited time to make their speech (your instructor will tell you how long each speaker has).

- The member of the team which proposes the motion (Team A) starts, followed by a member of the opposition (Team B) giving their speech, then back to Team A, until all have spoken.

- The last speaker in each team summarizes the discussion, including a rebuttal of what the opposite team has said.

- The discussion is then open to the floor, with any points the audience wishes to make.

- A vote by the judges decides the winning team.

5.4 **Now conduct the debate. Two teams should debate the motion, while the rest of the group acts as the audience and judges.**

Task 6: Perspectives on global issues

In the previous unit, you looked at finding a focus for a presentation and the need to develop your ideas around your focus. Task 6 gives further practice in developing this skill.

6.1 **Look at the following list of problems related to global issues.**

- The use of fossil fuels
- The credit crunch
- The wealth gap between developed and developing countries
- The spread of cyber-crime
- The spread of infectious diseases
- The disappearance of endangered languages

a) Think about the short- and long-term consequences of not dealing with each of these problems.

b) With a partner, discuss why it is important that solutions are found to each one.

Make notes in the table below on the consequences of each problem.

Problem	Consequences
The use of fossil fuels	
The credit crunch	
The wealth gap between developed and developing nations	
The spread of cyber-crime	
The spread of infectious diseases	
The disappearance of endangered languages	

6.2 In groups, choose one of the problems listed in Ex 6.1 and suggest some practical solutions for dealing with the problem. Do not complete the *evaluation* column yet.

Topic:	
Possible solutions	**Evaluation of solution**

6.3 Now look at your solutions and evaluate which are the most effective. This means considering:

- the advantages and disadvantages of each solution;
- what needs to be done to make each solution work;
- whether a suggested solution may create further problems.

a) Add some evaluative comments after each solution in the box in Ex 6.2.

b) Try to decide on the most effective way or ways of dealing with the problem.

6.4 As a group, take one problem and present it to the class. Include possible solutions and an evaluation of the solutions. Put your key ideas on an OHT.

The audience should try to ask questions at the end of each presentation.

Student's diary

- What did you learn in the unit about questionnaire design?
- Did you manage to identify the most important information from your data and present it clearly to your audience?
- In what way do you think your discussion skills have most improved on this course?
- Think about your role in the debate: What was the most challenging aspect of participation?

Unit Summary

In this unit you have designed a questionnaire and used it to collect and present information. You have also practiced debating global issues and considering and presenting solutions to environmental problems.

1   **In your notebook, complete the sentences below about designing and using questionnaires.**

Designing a questionnaire

- You should make sure you have a clear focus for your questionnaire.
- Your questions should be easy to understand and should elicit …
- Avoid questions that …

Administering a questionnaire

- Collect data by …
- Make sure your questions are clear by …

Presenting data that you have gathered

- Decide how …
- Highlight …
- Discuss …
- Evaluate …

---

2   **Think about the debates you have had in this unit. Discuss or think about the following questions.**

a)   What did you find most interesting and useful about taking part in a formal debate?

b)   What skills do feel you need to develop for a successful debate?

c)   How can debating skills help you in other areas of university life?

d)   Imagine you are going to debate the following motion: *The use of fossil fuels should be banned.*
What points could you make for and/or against the motion?

e)   Look at the following website: http://tnjn.com/2008/nov/16/students-debate-banning-of-fos/
Could you find any additional points that could be added to the debate?

For web resources relevant to this unit, see:
www.englishforacademicstudy.com/us/student/speaking/links

These weblinks will provide you with further information on global issues, ideas on how to carry out a survey and an insight into how students debate current issues.

9 Thinking Rationally
Science and the paranormal

In this unit you will:
- practice language for expressing differing degrees of belief;
- practice presenting a research proposal to a group of colleagues;
- consider the criteria for a good research proposal.

At university you are encouraged to think critically and take an analytical approach to issues. There is an emphasis on being able to explain things rationally. However, there are some issues that cannot be explained rationally, e.g., psychic phenomena. For many people, lack of a rational explanation does not make these phenomena any less real.

Task 1: The view of scientists

1.1 **Look at the following responses to the question: "What is the one thing everyone should learn about science?"**

a) Which statement comes closest to your belief about what science should teach?

b) Which of the statements appear to contradict one another? Which statements support one another?

1
> Science is about uncertainty. We do not yet know the answers to most of the most important questions.
>
> **Freeman Dyson, Emeritus Professor of Physics at the Institute for Advanced Study, Princeton.**

2
> I would teach the world that science is the best way to understand the world, and that for any set of observations, there is only one correct explanation.
>
> **Lewis Wolpert, Emeritus Professor of Biology as Applied to Medicine at University College London.**

3
> I would teach the world that scientists start by trying very hard to disprove what they hope is true ... a scientist always acknowledges the possibility of error, and is less likely to be mistaken than one who always claims to be right.
>
> **Anthony Hoare, Senior Researcher at Microsoft Corporation.**

4
> I would teach the world that science = imagination + humility.
>
> **Michael Baum, Emeritus Professor of Surgery and Visiting Professor of Medical Humanities at University College London.**

5
> Paranormal phenomena do not exist. Magic, witchcraft, mind-reading, clairvoyance, faith healing and similar practices do not work and never have worked.
>
> **Roderich Tumulka, Researcher in Physics at the Mathematics Institute at the University of Tubingen.**

1.2 Read the following quotation. Bearing in mind what you have read in Ex 1.1, do you share this view on the importance of truth?

> Truth is important, we value it. The whole basis for civilization is the quest for knowledge. Critical thinking and rational science are important in helping us determine what is true and false.

Source: (2002, July 11). Leading Edge.

1.3 Read the following statements. Then discuss your views on them with a partner.

a) During your discussion take into account any conclusions you have reached for Ex 1.1 and 1.2.

b) Try to give examples in support of your views.

> If a phenomenon cannot be proved scientifically, then we should not believe it.

> Some phenomena exist which science cannot explain.

Task 2: Beliefs that are contrary to scientific theory

Traditional beliefs relating to areas such as healing and medicine are common to all societies, whether or not the society as a whole subscribes to a scientific model.

2.1 Discuss these questions in groups.

a) What kinds of traditional beliefs are common in your country?

b) Are there some areas where people believe more in traditional medicine, or believe in phenomena such as witchcraft and magic?

2.2 Do you believe in any of the following phenomena? Use the *Useful language* expressions below to discuss your opinions.

| telepathy | ghosts/haunted houses | mind control | hypnosis | astrology |
| fortune-telling | UFOs | alien abductions | reincarnation | |

Useful language: Expressing doubt and belief

I don't believe in this/in these!	*It might be true …*
They don't exist.	*There might be something in it …*
It can't possibly be true …	*I believe it does/might work.*

2.3 What alternate explanations might there be for any of the phenomena in Ex 2.2?

Example:

Alien abductions: Many people claim to have been kidnapped by aliens. Here are some possible interpretations of these claims:

● the claims are true;

● people are lying, e.g., to gain attention;

● they are imagining it—it's a delusion;

● there is a scientific explanation, e.g., Chris French, head of psychology research at a London University, states that the experience is due to a condition known as "sleep paralysis." When this happens, people are temporarily trapped between being asleep and being awake, and cannot move. They often see and hear things which they are convinced are real.

Source: Sample, I. (2005, October 26). When sleep's an alien experience. *The Guardian*.

2.4 Work in groups and share what you know of any research that has attempted to prove whether any of the phenomena in Ex 2.2 are true or false.

Example:

To test the existence of telepathy, researchers at the University of Edinburgh put two subjects in separate sealed rooms. One subject was shown photographs and videos and tried to communicate these to the other subject. The other subject had to draw pictures of whatever came into their mind. Researchers looked to see if there was any statistically significant correspondence between the sent and received images.

2.5 In groups, choose one of the other phenomena in Ex 2.2 and discuss how you could test whether it exists or not. What type of experiment could you design?

2.6 Listen and comment on the experiments proposed by other groups.

Presentation skill: At higher levels of academic study, you may have to carry out some original research. You may have to present your research proposal to your professors and peers. Task 3 looks at these types of presentations.

Task 3: Designing and presenting a research paper

On your future academic courses, especially for graduate students, presenting a research proposal is common. This involves presenting what you plan to write about/research. Your colleagues and professors respond by commenting and giving feedback to help develop the proposal.

The type of presentation may vary according to the department you are in, so it is important to check the criteria expected by your particular department. Some academic disciplines or subjects do not lend themselves to experiment. Instead, these departments are better suited to writing a paper which relates theory to practice, and this is what you would present to colleagues.

3.1 Read the factors below that need to be considered when conducting an experiment. Then discuss the following questions in groups.

- experimental groups and control groups;
- number of subjects;
- statistical significance;
- variables;
- recommendations for further research.

a) Are such experiments carried out by people conducting research in your area of study?

b) If so, what kinds of theory are they hoping to prove/disprove?

3.2 Prepare a research proposal, either for an experiment or for a paper, according to your area of study.

a) Refer to the four headings listed below (these will vary according to the department where you study; if you have the criteria from your future department, you can use these headings) and make notes under each heading.

b) Rewrite your notes in a way that will best support you in your presentation. (Remember that you should deliver your presentation from notes.)

Title

Rationale for the study (Background information and the overall aim of the research.)

Proposed research questions (Specific questions which the research hopes to answer.)

Methods of data collection (This could include questionnaires, interviews, or simply collecting information from different sources.)

For a sample proposal, see Appendix 7.

3.3 Deliver the presentation to your group.

a) Take turns to give your presentation.

b) Listen to the proposals given by the rest of the group and evaluate the design of the proposal, e.g., are there any obvious weaknesses in the proposal? Use the audience feedback sheet in Appendix 9g.

3.4 Exchange feedback within your group.
Go through the feedback you have written on the audience feedback sheet. Complete and discuss feedback with one student before moving onto the next student.

Student's diary

- What did you learn from your discussions about scientific and non-scientific beliefs?
- How do you feel your presentation skills have developed up to this point?
- Do you require any further clarification from your instructor about making a research proposal?

In this unit you have practiced thinking critically and expressing personal beliefs. You have also practiced preparing and presenting a mini-research proposal.

1 **In your notebook, write answers to the questions below. Use the *Useful language* from the lesson.**

a) *Witchcraft exists and witches can do magic.* Do you believe this is true?

b) Do you believe that hypnosis is effective? What evidence is there that it does or doesn't work?

c) Do you believe that horoscopes and fortune-tellers can predict future events? How could this claim be tested?

d) Do you agree that some people can communicate with the dead? Give reasons for your belief.

2 **Read the following topic for a research proposal. Then think of how you could complete the proposal and make brief notes under each heading.**

Title: There is no clear correlation between gender and belief in the paranormal.

Rationale: It is a traditional belief that females are more superstitious than males …

Proposed research questions:

Subjects/sources of data:

Questionnaires/interviews:

Methods of data collection:

3 **Plan how to present the research proposal above. Practice presenting it to a partner.**

For web resources relevant to this unit, see:
www.englishforacademicstudy.com/us/student/speaking/links
This weblink will provide help with scientific words and expressions.

10

The Importance of Reflection
Studying in a new environment

In this unit you will:
● practice exchanging information;
● reflect on what you have gained from your time on this course;
● reflect on the skills you have developed on the course and how you can continue to develop them.

Many of you will have been settling into a new environment while using this book—a new college or university, perhaps in a new city or country. An important part of learning is reflection on your experience. You should regularly reflect on what you have learned and how you have learned it. It is useful to reflect on recent learning experiences, for example by writing a student's diary, as well as taking a longer perspective and reflecting on what you have learned over a whole course. This unit asks you to look at the long-term perspective of your learning experience.

Task 1: Looking back

1.1 **Think back over your first few weeks or months in this new environment and make notes on:**

a) two aspects of life that you have found surprising during your time here;

b) two aspects of life that you have enjoyed;

c) two aspects of life that you have found difficult.

1.2 **Discuss your notes with the class.**

Task 2: Stages of culture shock

A number of psychological studies claim that people's reactions tend to follow a common pattern while they are settling into a new environment.

2.1 **Read the descriptions in the table below of the five stages identified by Jane Woolfenden. Decide on their chronological order and number the stages 1–5.**

Stage no.	Description of stage
	You thought you had gotten used to it, but one or two minor things go wrong and it feels as if the whole world is against you. Some people give up at this stage, or become aggressive or withdrawn.
	Excitement.
	Adjustment to the new environment takes place. You either integrate into the new culture, or decide that you don't like it but have to tolerate it temporarily.
	You begin to get used to it.
	Culture shock. A few things start to go wrong. Differences between your own culture and the new culture start to cause problems. What was once new and exciting now seems unfamiliar and frustrating.

Source: Woolfenden, J. (1990). *How to study and live in Britain*. Northcote House.

2.2 Discuss your choices in Ex 2.1 with a partner. In what way is your experience:

a) similar to the model?

b) different from the model?

2.3 Identify the most difficult stage in the process. What advice would you give to someone going through this stage?

Task 3: Listening to cultural advice

3.1 🎧 17/18 You will listen to either Text 1 (Gulin) or Text 2 (Chris). These are both speakers who recently completed a degree at an American university. They discuss the challenges that international students face and offer advice to people who are about to start a course.

a) Work in two groups. One group will listen to Text 1 and the other will listen to Text 2.

b) As you listen, take notes on the advice given by the speaker. Afterwards you will have to explain it to someone who has not listened to it.

3.2 Check your notes with a partner who listened to the same text. Clarify any uncertainties that arise.

3.3 Work with someone who listened to the other text in Ex 3.1. Find out what advice was given in the other text and note the advice down.

> **Study tip**
>
> When your partner is summarizing information, wait for an appropriate break between points or sections and then make sure that you have understood the point(s).

3.4 Discuss the importance of each piece of advice given. Rank each piece of advice 1, 2, 3, etc. (1 = most important).

Task 4: Advice for international students

4.1 Read the following scenario and follow the instructions.

Some international students have just arrived in the town where you are staying. The students have got only three or four days to settle in before they start a 12-month course at the school or university where you are studying.

In groups, draft an advice sheet for the students. Use your notes from Ex 3.4 and your own experience as an international student to help you.

4.2 Transfer the main headings from your advice sheet to a poster, PowerPoint slide, or OHT.

4.3 One member of each group should present the group's advice sheet to the whole class, using the visual aid prepared in Ex 4.2.

4.4 With the other members of the class, decide which group's advice sheet would be the most useful for the newly arrived international students.

Task 5: Assessing your progress

5.1 Estimate your current level in each micro-skill listed in the following table. Put a check (✓) in the appropriate box (1 = poor; 5 = very good).

		1	2	3	4	5
1	I can use language appropriate to participation in a discussion, e.g., clarifying what someone has said, giving a counter-opinion.					
2	I can present an article to the class.					
3	I can lead a class (group discussion).					
4	I can participate confidently in a class discussion.					
5	I can put a point forward and develop my ideas.					
6	I can use a text to support my ideas.					
7	I can discuss an article and give my opinion in a class on pre-assigned articles I have read.					
8	I can build on what previous speakers have said in a discussion and add to it.					
9	I can plan an effective presentation.					
10	I can give a formal presentation using appropriate signposting.					
11	I can use PowerPoint effectively to support my presentation.					

5.2 Compare your completed tables with a partner or in small groups. In which areas do you feel you have made the most progress?

5.3 In your own time, look at Appendix 8 and underline those expressions that you remember using on this course.

Task 6: Ideas for future study

For some students, when you finish this course, your formal learning of English will draw to a close. However, there are still many areas of speaking English you need to develop. What are these areas, and how do you plan to keep working on them?

Area to work on	How to do this

Student's diary

Make an entry in your student's diary, with some concluding reflections on your progress in speaking on this course. You can base your entry on your responses to Tasks 5 and 6.

If you find it beneficial, continue using your diary after the course has finished. You can reflect on your further progress in English, particularly if you follow up your plans from Task 6.

For web resources relevant to this unit, see:
www.englishforacademicstudy.com/us/student/speaking/links

This weblink will provide you with comprehensive information on the theory behind cultural differences.

g Glossary

Acknowledge
To refer to someone else's idea or what someone has said and admit that it exists and/or recognize that it is true or valid.

Analytical approach
A way of looking at or presenting an argument. It involves analyzing ideas and concepts, discussing the issues and evaluating them before constructing a balanced argument.

Anticipate
To predict and prepare for an event. In academic life it is important to anticipate what someone will say in a lecture, what they will argue in a class, and what questions they will ask.

Appoint (chairperson)
To choose (formally) someone to do a job or take a role in a situation such as a meeting or debate.

Challenge (an assumption) (v)
To question or oppose an idea that you or others have assumed to be true, but not really examined thoroughly.

Claim (v, n)
To state that something is true but not have clear evidence or proof that it is a fact.

Contradict
To oppose a statement or situation. If you state the opposite of what someone else has said, you are contradicting them. New evidence which does not support a previous claim can also contradict it.

Controversial
Something that is disputed. People often argue about or debate controversial topics such as stem-cell research.

Counter-argument
The opposite argument to the one already stated.

Critical reading
Reading in a way that involves questioning what the text says, what the writer is trying to do, and how he or she does this.

Critical thinking skills
Thinking critically involves the following skills: supporting your own views with a clear rationale, evaluating ideas that you hear and read, and making connections between ideas.

Dominate (a discussion)
To control a discussion and have a strong influence over it; or to spend more time talking than others in the group.

Excerpt
A short extract or part of a recording or written text.

Impact
An effect or strong impression.

Issue
A problem, topic, or area for discussion that needs to be worked on.

Learning style
The way that someone learns best, e.g., students can have analytical, global, or communicative learning styles. They are also sometimes said to have visual, auditory, or kinesthetic (sensory) learning styles.

Outcome (of a discussion)
The result or agreed conclusion that follows a discussion, meeting, or set of events.

Overview (of a topic)

A summary of the key points of a topic or area that is to be discussed. The overview may list the main areas to talk/think about or give a brief introduction to them.

Perspective

A point of view. In academic life, looking at an issue from different perspectives is part of the process of reaching a balanced conclusion.

Pilot (v)

To try something out for the first time to make sure that it works correctly, e.g., a book, a test, a questionnaire, or a program. Adaptations may be made after the piloting stage.

Prioritize

To rank items or points in order of importance, e.g., someone may need to prioritize their work, ideas, or plans.

Qualify (a statement)

To give further explanation about a statement, e.g., to state the conditions where it applies, e.g., *this action should only be taken in extreme cases* ... is an example of a qualifying statement.

Rebuttal

Expressing evidence that destroys the opposing evidence, or an argument that goes against a previous argument. Speakers in a debate have to give a rebuttal of the other team's arguments.

Signpost language

Functional word(s) and/or phrase(s) that help to structure a spoken or written text and show the listener or reader where the speaker is going. For example, forward signposts may refer to what the speaker or writer is going to say next, e.g., *First I want to... then ... finally.*

Speaking turns

In a conversation, turn-taking refers to the way that people speak when they have an opportunity and how they pass the floor to another person through, e.g., a glance, gesture, or speech pause.

Strategy

Something that you can do to improve a skill, or to deal with a challenging situation over a period of time. Useful strategies for improving class participation include asking questions to check understanding and asking for clarification.

Subscribe to

If you subscribe to an opinion or idea, you agree to it and openly adopt it as a belief.

ENTREPRENEUR PLANS
A FREE GLOBAL UNIVERSITY
THAT WILL BE ONLINE ONLY

AN entrepreneur with decades of experience in international education plans to start the first global, tuition-free Internet university, a nonprofit project he has named the University of the People.

5 **"THE** open-source courseware is there, from universities that have put their courses online, available to the public, free," Mr. Reshef said. "We know that online peer-to-peer teaching works. Putting it all together, we can make a free university for students all over the world, for anyone who speaks
10 English and has an Internet connection."

ABOUT four million students in the United States took at least one online course in 2007, according to a survey into mainstream higher education. Online learning is growing in many different contexts. Through the Open Courseware
15 Consortium, started in 2001 by the Massachusetts Institute of Technology, universities around the world have posted materials for thousands of courses all free to the public. Many universities now post their lectures on iTunes.

THE University of the People, like other Internet-based
20 universities, would have online study communities, weekly discussion topics, homework assignments and exams. But instead of tuition, students would pay only nominal fees for enrollment and exams, with students from poorer countries paying the lower fees and those from richer countries paying
25 the higher ones.

MR. Reshef said his new university would use active and retired professors along with librarians, Masters-level students and professionals to develop and evaluate curriculums and oversee assessments. He plans to start small, limiting
30 enrollment at 300 students when the university goes online in the fall and offering only bachelor's degrees in business administration and computer science. Mr. Reshef said the university would apply for accreditation as soon as possible. He hopes to build enrollment to 10,000 over five years, the
35 level at which he said the enterprise should be self-sustaining.

Speaking & Pronunciation

E FOR DEGREE

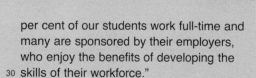

Online studying is allowing graduates to continue in education while working

By Stephen Hoare

Graduates in the UK wanting to study for a further qualification no longer have to delay their entry into the job market and the opportunity to start
5 **repaying their student loans.**

Many are opting to study for a masters degree or graduate qualification online, enabling them to combine study with a full-time career.

10 *The Guardian*'s education website reveals a number of universities offering online graduate courses in business, electronic commerce, internet systems development, online education and even sociology—
15 areas that make heavy use of internet technology. Most are at masters or diploma level.

The biggest online provider is the UK-based Open University, which has more
20 than 30,000 graduates worldwide and offers 63 courses online. OU pro-vice-chancellor, Professor Linda Jones, says: "Online links generally with the advantages of Open University study.
25 Students can be very flexible and fit study around personal circumstances. Over 70 per cent of our students work full-time and many are sponsored by their employers, who enjoy the benefits of developing the
30 skills of their workforce."

The OU has discovered that take-up of online graduate degrees is enhanced by technical support such as online conferencing and student discussion
35 groups, as well as an efficient online registration and tracking system. All online students are offered personal tutorials.

Online and distance learning provider Pearson Education runs the highly
40 successful Herriot-Watt business school MBA, and has teamed up with Portsmouth University to offer an online MSc in internet systems development. Now entering their second year, the Portsmouth online
45 graduate courses have attracted mainly UK students, but with growing numbers from Africa and Asia.

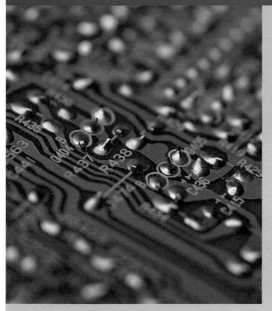

certificate courses such as the certificate in online learning offered by London University's Institute of Education.

75 Senior lecturer Anita Pincas says: "Online study makes it so much easier to deal with the huge numbers of students on today's campus. There's no way the professor can see everyone. Plus it's very
80 difficult for students to collaborate with each other if they are busy with classes. Virtual meetings add to what students can do."

Some online graduate courses offer
85 students access to information that might prove difficult to research if all they had available was the university library. The University of Surrey management school's online MBA has links to the
90 university's learning resources department, a full range of academic journals and even Reuters business information. Commercial director Chris Croker says: "We give our students a
95 laptop pre-loaded with all the multimedia course material, access to over 1,400 management journals and even access to our students' union. The only thing they can't do is buy a round of drinks!"

A spokesperson for Pearson's distributed learning division says: "We have identified
50 e-courses as a growth area and the courses we have developed with Portsmouth appeal mainly to people who are working. Most are on a career path and have been out of full-time education
55 for several years."

With the university taking care of course content and the accreditation, and Pearson adding marketing expertise, an internet platform and technical support,
60 Portsmouth's online students benefit from tried and tested distance learning techniques. Online also has the added advantage of enabling academics to update course material. A spokesperson
65 says: "Being online allows us to update once or twice a semester."

Advantages vary, but a major attraction is flexibility. Students can complete an online degree over a longer timespan—
70 possibly taking a mix and match of units. Online is also suited to short but intensive

E FOR DEGREE

Source: Hoare, S. (2003, August 26). E for Degree. *The Guardian.*

New "DADITUDE"
Today's fathers are hands-on

Today's fathers may take parenting as seriously as their mates, but unlike many moms, dads don't view it as a competitive sport.
5 Instead, the new attitude of 21st-century fatherhood is hands-on and involved, but with a hint of playfulness.

"All of these social expectations
10 have developed over decades about what moms are supposed to do. We don't have a new picture of what involved dads are supposed to look like," says Will Courtenay, a
15 psychotherapist in Berkeley, Calif., who is on the advisory board of The Center for Men and Young Men at McLean Hospital, Harvard Medical School.

20 Those who study fatherhood say today's dads are forging a new identity, as working women press for a more egalitarian home life. Telecommuting and workplace flexibility are making it
25 possible for dads to have more time with the kids. Also, dads today are no longer the stuffy or clueless fathers portrayed on TV. "It's cool now to be an active, involved father," says Aaron
30 Rochlen, associate professor of psychology at the University of Texas-Austin. "Overall, men being more active fathers is starting to become the norm and less of an anomaly."

35 As a result, there has been a real shift in the way men talk about fatherhood,

experts say: Young dads (generally those in their early 40s and younger) say they know they're not perfect, but
40 they don't worry about being judged. Compared with pressure that many moms say they feel, "the bar is set pretty low for father involvement and father engagement," says Jeff Cookston,
45 an assistant professor of psychology who studies fatherhood at San Francisco State University. He calls the current group of younger dads a "pilot generation" because they're trying to
50 figure out the transition from dad as a breadwinner to the hands-on pop who doesn't shirk from diaper changes or carpool runs.

Psychiatrist Kyle Pruett of the Yale
55 University Child Study Center in New Haven, Conn., has seen lots of changes in more than 25 years teaching child development. When he started, his students were all girls. "Now, we've had
60 a couple of years where there were male majorities, including one year where the entire starting line of the hockey team came to the class," he says.

English for academic study

Teen births decline

Researchers are alarmed by an increase in out-of-wedlock pregnancies. A new federal report on birth statistics shows a "thrilling" 12-year decline in teen births - and a "very alarming"
5 jump in the portion of births that occur out of wedlock.

The report, "Births: Preliminary Data For 2003," released yesterday shows "two competing trends," said Wade F. Horn,
10 assistant secretary for children and families at the Department of Health and Human Services. "The report shows that we are doing a much better job at convincing young people that it's not a good idea to have, or
15 father, a child while you're a teenager," said Mr. Horn, referring to the 3 percent drop in teen births from 2002 to 2003. At the same time, he said, the rise in giving birth to children out of wedlock to 34.6 percent
20 shows "that we still need to do a better job at helping people understand that there are advantages to waiting until you're married to become a parent."

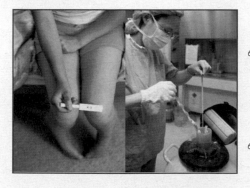

Other highlights from the new birth report,
25 released by the National Center for Health Statistics (NCHS), are a marked 6 percent increase in births by Caesarean-section delivery and increases in births among older mothers. In 2003, for the first time, births to
30 women ages 40 or older topped 100,000 in a single year, said a spokesman for the Centers for Disease Control and Prevention, which oversees the NCHS.

The latest 3 percent drop in teen births is
35 "simply thrilling," said Sarah Brown, director of the National Campaign to Prevent Teen Pregnancy. Teen birthrates have fallen 33 percent since their 1991 peak, and this represents "a very profound change in
40 America," she said. To Heritage Foundation analyst Robert Rector, the more important— and "very alarming"—number is the portion of unwed births, which has risen from 33.5 percent in 2001 to 34.6 percent in 2003.
45 When it comes to child poverty and other family problems, he said, "it does not matter much" whether a woman is 18 or 20, when she has a child out of wedlock. "What matters is whether she's married at the time at birth."

50 The unwed-birth data, however, didn't worry Marshall Miller, a co-founder of the Alternatives to Marriage Project in Albany, N.Y., a group for unmarried persons. "If you just read numbers on a paper, you don't know
55 why people decide to have a child or marry or not," Mr. Marshall said. "I think hand-wringing about births to unmarried parents, as opposed to looking at what's going on in their lives, misses the point," he said, adding
60 that many unwed births are to older, single career women who have chosen to have a child, long-term cohabiting couples and same-sex couples who can't "marry."

Other highlights of the NCHS report:
65 • The number of US births rose by less than 1 percent, to 4.1 million.
• The number of unwed births rose from 1,365,966 in 2002 to 1,415,804 in 2003.
• The teen birthrate of 41.7 births per 1,000
70 teens in 2003 marks a 33 percent decline in teen birthrates since 1991.
• The youngest group of mothers, ages 10 to 14, had 6,665 births in 2003—the fewest in 45 years.
75 • Women in their late 20s remain the most likely to have babies (115.7 births per 1,000 women ages 25 to 29).

Source: Wetzstein, C. (2004, November 24). Teen births decline, report shows. *The Washington Times.*

TIME

All but the Ring:

Why Some Couples Don't Wed

For well over a year, I campaigned for my boyfriend and me to wed. "I don't see what the point of marriage is," he'd say. Eventually I gave up and moved on to the next topic: babies. "Absolutely," he replied. We'd been together for 2½ years by that point, and while he didn't want to bother getting married, a family was something he could happily commit to.

It turns out he's in good company. More than 5 million unmarried couples cohabit in the US, nearly eight times the number in 1970, and a record-breaking 40% of babies born in 2007 had unmarried parents, up 25% from 2002. Nonmarital births have increased the most among women ages 25 to 39, doubling since 1980, thanks in part to a small but growing demographic a sociologist has dubbed committed unmarrieds (CUs). These are the happily unwed whose commitment to their partners is as strong as their stance against marriage.

Celebrities, gay-marriage bans and fear of divorce are helping fuel the rise in unwedded bliss. "We love each other far, far too much to ever get married," says Raymond McCauley, 43, who lives in California with his twin 2-year-olds and his partner of five years, Kristina Hathaway. Instead of a marriage license, he and Hathaway have drawn up legal documents that grant them rights automatically given to married couples, covering everything from child custody to property. And yet this arrangement still gives him some sense of freedom. "Every day we're making this decision and this commitment anew," he says. "I'm not with you because there would be legal speed bumps to get through if we weren't. I'm with you because this is where I want to be."

"You're looking at the vanguard," sociologist Andrew Cherlin says of CUs like McCauley and Hathaway. A Johns Hopkins professor and author of *The Marriage-Go-Round: The State of Marriage and the Family in America Today*, he notes that unmarried parents in Europe stay together longer than married parents in the US. "Marriage is a more powerful symbol here," he says. "It's the ultimate merit badge of personal life." And if it doesn't fulfill people's expectations, 55 they leave.

Indeed, a study published in the December *Journal of Marriage and Family* found that a man's involvement in his partner's pregnancy —trips to the doctor, childbirth classes, etc. — 60 was the best way to secure his long-term dedication. Lead author Natasha Cabrera of the University of Maryland says, "It is the decision that couples make to strengthen commitment and move in together that is 65 important, rather than marital status per se."

Marriage can always end, and the protection it once offered offspring is now covered by child-support laws. Add that development to the gains made by the domestic-partnership 70 movement, "and the legal advantages of marriage are eroding," Cherlin says. This is one reason CUs like Charles Backman, 44, a commercial real estate developer in New Hampshire, see marriage as outdated at best. 75 Backman wants no part of what he calls "the government stamp" of approval on his relationship to his partner of 15 years. "People mistake government sanction of your marriage for commitment," he says. The 80 father of three girls ages one to seven, Backman finds marriage not only unnecessary but also tarnished by commercialization.

Of course, "unmarriage" isn't a guarantee of 85 love everlasting any more than marriage. According to Rutgers University's National Marriage Project, cohabiting couples are at least twice as likely to break up as married couples are. Long term, notes Stephanie 90 Coontz, a professor of history and family studies at Washington's Evergreen State

College, unmarriage works only if both people are equally committed to the lack of legal commitment. If not, to borrow a phrase from 95 Beyoncé: "If you like it, then you should have put a ring on it."

The majority of cohabitants either break up or marry within five years, says Alison Hatch, a grad student at the University of Colorado 100 who is doing her dissertation on committed unmarrieds, a demographic to which she and her partner of six years belong. She and Coontz have found that many of them end up marrying because they face the same 105 discrimination as gay couples regarding insurance, taxes and other legal issues. Having kids can also change things. David Letterman didn't say what prompted him to wed his partner of 23 years, who is also the 110 mother of his 5-year-old son. "I know that in our case, the plus sign on my pregnancy test led my boyfriend and me to marry in April, which has made our relationship feel more committed, but maybe a little less cool."

MARRIED-WITH-CHILDREN STILL FADING

Census Finds Americans Living Alone in 25% of Households

The number of Americans living alone grew rapidly in the 1990s, for the first time surpassing the number of married couples with children, according to recent census data. These point to the redefinition of the American household in recent
5 decades and the shrinking dominance of married-with-children families. Among the fastest-growing groups were unmarried partners whose numbers rose 72 percent over the decade. The nation's count of single-father households went up 62 percent, although single mothers still far outnumber them.

10 The new figures are the first from the 2000 Census to provide a statistical overview of how Americans live, their household circumstances and the shape of their families. The statistics showed no reversal of a decades-long national trend away from the historically dominant household, married
15 couples with children. That change is a result of divorce as well as Americans choosing to wed later or not at all and, in some cases, not having children.

These trends continued in the '90s but the pace of change slowed. Earlier numbers also showed a recent leveling-off of
20 US rates for divorce and unmarried births. "The central place of marriage in our family system is eroding," said Andrew J. Cherlin, a Johns Hopkins University sociology professor. "Secondly, Americans are using their greater affluence for expressing their preference for living alone."

In past head counts, the Washington area has ranked above the national
25 average in the share of people living alone, single parents and unmarried couples. Figures released recently show that the nation's 54.5 million married couples, with or without children, now make up barely half of American households. Meanwhile, nearly a third of the nation's 105 million households are occupied by single people without children, roommates, live-in couples and
30 other unrelated people. In 1940, less than 8 percent of all households consisted of people living alone; now, more than a quarter do. That is one reason why the nation's average household size hit a record low in 2000, 2.59 people.

The number of "unmarried partners," an option first provided on the 1990 Census form, has grown to more than 5.4
35 million, according to the new figures. Details are not available on gender makeup, but a decade ago, most were male-female couples. The number of live-in couples is increasing among all age groups, a rise that is increasingly influencing companies and governments to offer benefits and extend legal protections to
40 unmarried partners. A growing share of unmarried partners— at least a third—have children living with them, according to other surveys. Most single fathers live with another adult, generally a female partner or female relative, according to surveys, though most single mothers do not.

45 Demographers studying the trend have wondered whether the United States would become more like Europe, where unmarried couples often live together for decades while raising children. So far, though, studies show a greater proportion of American live-in couples break up, which causes instability in children's lives, said Brown University sociology professor Frances Goldscheider.
50

LIVING TOGETHER NO LONGER 'PLAYING HOUSE'

A generation ago, unmarried couples who lived together were often looked down on for "shacking up" or "playing house." Studies in the 1980s supported those negative stereotypes, suggesting that cohabitation could damage
5 a long-term relationship and substantially raise the risk of divorce.

While researchers say the overall divorce rate is higher among those who lived together before marriage, now they don't blame cohabitating. "There's been a big
10 change in societal, cultural and individual acceptance of cohabitation," says Pamela Smock, a sociologist at the Population Studies Center at the University of Michigan-Ann Arbor. "A lot of the earlier studies were relying on data that may have come from the late '80s and mid-
15 '90s. The evidence is a lot more mixed."

Researchers say changing times have produced more extensive information about cohabitaters and more sophisticated research methods. Recent census data show 9.6% of all opposite-sex couples living together in
20 2007 were unmarried. "Cohabitation has become a common experience in people's lives," Smock says.

"The nature of cohabitation has changed," says Jay Teachman, a sociology professor at Western Washington University in Bellingham. "Cohabitators 20 years ago
25 were the rule breakers, the rebels, the risk takers—the folks who were not as interested in marriage." He pointed out that twenty or 25 years ago, "if you were cohabitating and then married, the marriage was more likely to dissolve and end in divorce," he says. "Today,
30 that's not the case. You can cohabitate with your spouse and not experience increased risk of divorce."

Those aren't the only studies reflecting changes—researchers across the country, including at the University of Wisconsin, the University of Minnesota,
35 Cornell University and others, are studying cohabitating couples. Among other recent findings:

- The odds of divorce among women who married their only cohabitating partner were 28% lower than among women who never cohabitated before marriage,
40 according to sociologist Daniel Lichter of Cornell University in Ithaca, N.Y.
- Divorce rates for those who cohabitate more than once are more than twice as high as for women who cohabitated only with their eventual husbands.
45 - Cohabitating between a first and second marriage doesn't raise the risk of divorce—unless the woman brings a child into the marriage from a previous relationship. A man with a child from a previous relationship does not raise the likelihood of a second
50 divorce.

Other recent studies have shown that certain subgroups don't appear to experience negative effects from co-habitating, such as engaged couples who move in together. Some new research goes further, suggesting
55 that living together may reduce risk of divorce. "We showed women who only cohabitated with their husband had lower rates of divorce than women who went straight to marriage," Lichter says. "There seems to be less risk than if you cohabitate many times or if you don't
60 cohabitate at all." His research on serial cohabitation analyzed data from the National Longitudinal Survey of Youth and found that women living with even one more man in a romantic relationship other than the eventual spouse increased divorce risk.

65 Sociologist Kelly Musick, also from Cornell, says the focus on cohabitation research is shifting. "The emphasis used to be on trying to understand why couples who cohabitate before marriage split up at higher rates than those who don't," she says. "More recent studies have tried to
70 understand more about what it means and look at it more as a family form in its own right."

Source: Jayson, S. (2008, July 28). Living together no longer 'playing house'. USA TODAY

Real fathers fail to measure up to televised versions

Today's fathers feel like failures after losing their traditional role as head of the family. Many admit that they are worse parents than their fathers, that
5 **they avoid emotional involvement with their children and use the office to avoid the stress of their home life.**

"Fatherhood is becoming a mild form of depression for the modern-day man, there is a grey cloud that hangs over it," said Marian Salzman, chief strategy officer at the advertising and public relations company Euro RSCG Worldwide. "Society offers no realistic role models for real men trying to do their best," said Salzman. "The disappointment and feeling of failure is resulting in men shutting down emotionally because they no longer have the old central role in their family and don't know what other role is available for them."

Fathers in the US are a lot less supportive and accepting than TV sitcom dads, even falling short
10 of the low bar set by Homer Simpson, a study of college students' views suggests. Many young people blame constant work demands—rarely shown on TV—for draining their fathers' energy and time from parenting, says Janice Kelly, a
15 communications researcher at Marymount Manhattan College in New York. She showed episodes from eight comedies to 108 college students. The programs were as diverse as The *George Lopez Show, The Simpsons, My Wife and*
20 *Kids* and *Everyone Loves Raymond*. She asked the students to rate TV fathers and their own on such qualities as support, guidance, acceptance of other family members and oppositional behavior (for example, ridiculing children). On every
25 measure, TV fathers were rated significantly better than the students' own dads.

Comments invited during the study were revealing, Kelly says. One young person wrote: "My father works two jobs to support the family. I
30 don't get to see him, when he comes home he's tired." Children from white-collar families portrayed their fathers as tied to BlackBerrys and e-mail, afraid of losing their jobs. "One girl said: 'That's why he makes pancakes on the weekend.
35 He feels guilty,'" Kelly says. Everyone knows TV isn't life, "but still, the real dad is being judged poorly compared to these television daddies," says Glenn Good, an expert in the psychology of men at the University of Missouri. "There's a lot of
40 research showing these programs can create norms of what's right."

Many fathers see holding on to jobs as key to good parenting of their kids, he adds, "but it's a challenging economic time." Men's real income
45 from all sources fell from 2000 to 2005, according to US government figures. "Several studies confirm that fathers are spending more time than ever on child care," says Vincent DiCaro of the non-profit National Fatherhood
50 Initiative. "It's unknown whether Gen X and Y fathers—born between 1965 and 1994—will be seen as more nurturing than baby-boom fathers," DiCaro says. "There's very little research on the parenting of earlier generations of men," he
55 says.

Kelly says TV writers should show more of this true-life work/family conflict. "But that won't happen," says Robert Thompson, director of the Bleier Center for Television and Popular Culture at
60 Syracuse University. "Working families are having a hard enough time balancing child care and jobs. Do you want to sit down and watch this at night? Most people would run away screaming."

To the contrary, Thompson says, family sitcoms
65 already "are on life support," fast disappearing, because stressed-out viewers crave "anesthesia" in over-the-top "reality" and other escapist shows. "It's disturbing to think that kids might judge their dad as worse than Homer Simpson,"
70 he says. "Ward Cleaver was one thing—nobody could measure up—but sitcom dads today are flawed at best."

'Society is alienating fathers from their children'

Source: Elias, M. (2007, June 13).
Study: Real fathers fail to measure
up to televised versions.
USA TODAY

Affluent
but Anxious
and Alienated

Will Woodward

A far-reaching survey over decades finds Britons better off but more unhappy.

Despite higher incomes, better health and much greater opportunity for women, Britons are increasingly depressed,
5 unhappy in their relationships, and alienated from civic society, according to an exhaustive study to be published next week.

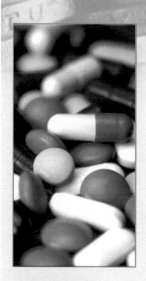

The latest findings come from three pioneering studies, which have been following the lives of everyone born in England, Scotland and Wales in one week in 1946, 1958 and 1950—more
10 than 40,000 people.

The study, Changing Britain, Changing Lives, is the first to compare in detail the results of the three studies. It identifies a society more fractured and individualistic, but where people at the same time find their success, wealth and opportunity
15 dependent on family background to an even greater extent.

Fourteen percent of men born in 1970 were as likely to admit to depression and anxiety in 2000, compared with only seven percent of the 1958 group in 1991. For women the differences in the same years were almost as dramatic—20 percent in
20 2000 and 12 percent in 1991.

Of those born in 1970, 22 percent of men and 24 percent of women admitted to being unhappy with their first marriage in their early 30s, compared with just three percent of men and two percent of women of those born in 1958 at the same age.
25 Single people too were similarly much more likely to be unhappy with their lives.

Those born later stay in the family home for longer periods because of the rising cost of housing. They also increasingly delay parenthood until their late 30s and early 40s, at a point
30 when their own parents become in need of support. They then have to look after their own children and support their parents at the same time, and are unlikely to enjoy the extended period of freedom from dependency enjoyed by adults in the past.

Ninety percent of women and 80 percent of men among the 1946
35 group had become parents by the age of 30. However, this was
true of only 30 percent of men and 52 percent of women among
those born in 1970.

The "striking increase" in women entering higher education
and establishing themselves in the labour market has led to
40 relationships and parenthood coming later. Three-quarters of
30-year-old women were in employment in 2000, compared
with half of those aged 32 in 1978.

Average female earnings were almost twice as high for 30-year-
olds born in 1970 than for those born in 1946, although most
45 top jobs still went to men. The growing financial independence
of women also "means that economic considerations were less
likely to force them to remain in unhappy partnerships".

Women transformed their position, obtaining more higher
qualifications and staying on in education longer than men by
50 1970. Across both sexes, the percentages gaining a degree
quadrupled between the 1946 and 1970 groups, while the
proportions leaving with no qualifications plummeted from
40 percent to 10 percent.

But in education and employment, class remained a dominant
55 factor. "Those at the bottom end of the socioeconomic scale
manifested little evidence of the rising standards enjoyed by
the majority," the study says.

Rising house prices put owner-occupation out of reach, and
relative poverty was increasing. The study concludes: "Our
60 findings give few grounds for optimism that these disparities
are disappearing, or even diminishing. Despite rising education
levels and rising affluence ... the old polarities based on social
class appear, if anything to be strengthening."

Source: Woodward, W. (2003, February 22). Affluent but anxious
and alienated. *The Guardian.*

THE latest research on babies and how their brains develop shows that the attention that we receive as babies impacts
5 on our brain structures. If we find ourselves cared for by people who love us, and who are highly sensitive to our unique personalities, the
10 pleasure of those relationships will help to trigger the development of the "social brain". In the simplest terms, the prefrontal cortex (and in
15 particular its orbitofrontal area) plays a major role in managing our emotional lives: it picks up on social cues, the non-verbal messages
20 that other people transmit; it enables us to empathize, as well as playing an important part in restraining our primitive emotional impulse.

25 Surprising as it may seem, we are not born with these capacities: this part of the brain develops almost entirely post-natally. Nor is it just a
30 matter of waiting for your baby to develop an orbitofrontal cortex so it can

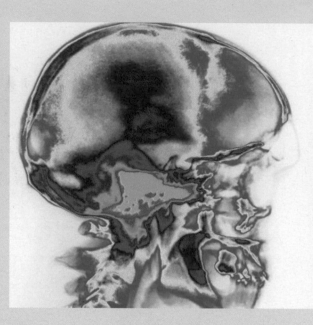

Cradle of civilization

begin to relate well to others. There is nothing automatic about it. Instead, the kind of brain that each baby develops is the brain
35 that comes out of his or her experiences with other people. Love facilitates a massive burst of connections in this part of the brain between six and 12 months. Neglect at this time can greatly reduce the development of the pre-frontal cortex.

Early care also establishes the way we deal with stress. Babies
40 rely on their carers to soothe distress and restore equilibrium. With responsive parents, the stress response, a complex chain of biochemical reactions, remains an emergency response. However, being with caregivers who convey hostility or resentment at a baby's needs, or who ignore their baby or leave him in a state
45 of distress for longer than he can bear, will make a baby's stress response over-sensitive. Recent research by Marilyn Essex at the University of Wisconsin shows that children who lived with a depressed parent in infancy are more reactive to stress later in life; children who lived with a depressed parent later in
50 childhood showed no such effect.

This makes sense in evolutionary terms to have newborn brains which are unfinished, because they can be adapted to fit the needs of the social group. In effect, they can be programmed to behave in ways that suit their community. However, it is a risky
55 strategy. In a harsh environment, a baby's cries may be ignored,

or he may be punished for being distressed. This is likely to produce an individual who becomes, in his turn, relatively insensitive and prone to aggression – and this could be useful in a tense, hostile community. Researchers have found clear links between harsh
60 treatment in the first two years and later antisocial behaviour.

This research has relevance to two current debates – on smacking and nurseries. Looked at from this perspective, one can clearly see that smacking is damaging. Furthermore, nurseries may not provide the things that babies need most: being held and
65 cuddled; having someone familiar and safe to notice how you feel, someone who can quickly put things right when they go wrong, someone who smiles at you lovingly. On the contrary, it is likely that babies in a nursery will find that they are not special to anyone in that way that parents believe their own children are,
70 and they will have to wait for attention. One close observational study of a local authority nursery found that there was little or no eye contact, and little holding or comforting.

The research bears out the effects of such nurseries on babies. Babies can only cope with about ten hours a week of daycare
75 before it may start to affect their emotional development, particularly if the care is of low quality. The strongest research findings are that full-time care during the first and second years is strongly linked to later behaviour problems. These are the children who are "mean" to others, who hit and blame other
80 children. They are likely to be less cooperative and more intolerant of frustration. These are all capacities which suggest poor development of the "social brain". Evidence that increasing the caregiver/baby ratio in nurseries does reduce problems of aggression confirms that these children have simply not had
85 enough loving, individual attention.

- -

These findings are not good news for working parents or for single parents who want to return to work. These parents may end up putting their babies into poor-quality, full-time nursery care before the age of six months. It is their children whose emotional and social development could be affected—not those of better-off parents who can afford to work part-time or buy in the highest
90 quality care. This is not a solution that benefits society in the long-term. The science is there, demonstrating the vulnerability of a baby's neurobiology; and the social research is there, showing that full-time nurseries are bad for babies.

It is time to think clearly about what our new options might be. Most women don't want to return to an age of mandatory full-time motherhood, especially given the stress and loneliness of being
95 at home with only a baby for company.

On the other hand, we can't afford not to provide the kind of loving one-on-one nurturing that babies need, if we want to have a cooperative, socially skilled society. Most mothers and an increasing number of fathers want to be able to spend time with their babies, and often feel that they lose touch with their babies if they work full-time.

100 We have to come up with new flexible solutions, such as extended paid parental leave, that enable both parents to be involved with their baby while keeping the family economy afloat. We need to ensure that our nurseries are of the highest quality. We also need more community involvement to prevent early parenthood from being isolated and miserable. By investing our time and money in the first two years of life, we will be repaid in greater social stability.

Source: Gerhardt, S. (2004, July 24). Cradle of Civilization. *The Guardian*.

Speaking & Pronunciation

US anti-obesity efforts found wanting

State and Federal governments have not placed enough emphasis on health and nutrition education

Researchers and public health advocates agree that efforts by the federal government and food industry to encourage healthier lifestyles have not slowed the rising trend of obesity in Americans. But nutritional experts, speaking at a panel held at the American Enterprise Institute, differ on
5 whom to blame or how to handle America's weight problem, which some have called an "epidemic."

Food industry officials have tried to head off government regulation and litigation with voluntary menu changes and labeling. The panel came after a recent decision by the 2nd U.S. Circuit Court of Appeals to reinstate part
10 of a lawsuit against McDonald's Corp. The suit was brought by New York teenagers who said McDonald's food and its misleading advertisements caused their obesity.

Some economists blamed expanding waistlines on declining food prices, more ready-to-eat food products, and a shift to more sedentary
15 employment. "We were paid in the past to exercise as part of our job, but now that has flipped and we are the ones paying to exercise," said Tomas Philipson, a University of Chicago professor and adviser to the Centers for Medicare and Medicaid Services.

The reality of more women in the work force has also altered how families,
20 often short of time, are getting their meals—with many families opting for restaurant and ready-made meals, said Jonathan Klick, a Florida State University assistant law professor. While acknowledging some progress in combatting obesity, Northeastern University professor Richard Daynard stressed that nutritional labeling on restaurant menus and stricter
25 regulation on advertising to children are needed. He suggested that a tax on "unhealthy" food and litigation against restaurants and food manufacturers may also help reduce consumption of fatty foods. Alison Rein, assistant director for food and health policy for the National Consumers League, said the obesity problem also stems from heavy
30 advertising from the food industry, primarily with ads targeting children.

About 15 percent of American children are overweight, while 64 percent of US adults are overweight or obese, according to the Centers for Disease Control and Prevention. Ms. Rein said state and federal governments have not placed enough emphasis on health and nutrition education.

35 "Obese people have pushed up health care costs while cutting into the work force's full production potential," said Ms. Rein. Mr. Philipson and other economists countered that obese people, like smokers, tend to die younger than the rest of the population, costing the government health care dollars but saving on Social Security pensions.

Source: Higgins, M. (2005, March 4). U.S. anti-obesity efforts found wanting. *The Washington Times*.

Stress is a part of our lives. Although there may be people who have less stress than others, we'd be hard pressed to find anyone who doesn't experience it. Ways of dealing with stress and keeping it at bay vary but some busy professionals are doing just that.

Stress

Exercise, hobbies, small rituals can ease stress

The causes of stress

Keith Bates of Madison has worked for 22 years in the hectic world of advertising. As a senior vice president with Marls, West & Baker of Jackson, Bates supervises account services in addition to the day-to-day

5 management of some accounts. His long time interest in cars, listening to smooth jazz, running and lifting weights keep him on an even keel. "Running allows you quality 'me time.' You're totally alone with your thoughts," he said. "I've solved many issues while

10 running at 6 a.m. Waxing and polishing my car is a labour of love. Perhaps best of all, it requires very little brain power. It's also very gratifying, especially if you're a little obsessive/ compulsive."

In addition to driving a 1998 Corvette, the 51-year-old

15 Bates collects toy cars, is a member of the Mississippi Classic Cruisers car club and is cofounder of a classic car show in Madison. "I love collecting toy cars. My mother once told me I would out grow them, but I never did and I hope I never do," he said. Bates, who

20 earned an art degree from Mississippi State University, enjoys running in 5K and 10K events too. Two of his most memorable races included running across the Mississippi River Bridge and through the hills of the Vicksburg Military Park. "My running career will be

25 complete when I run across the Golden Gate Bridge," he said.

Running also plays a major role in managing stress for Dr. Eugene McNally, a family practitioner in Gulfport.

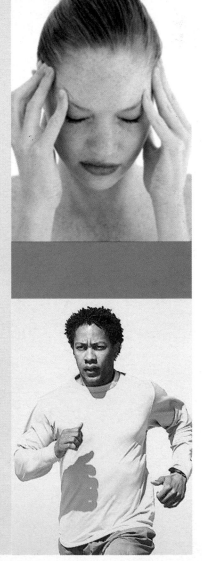

"Exercise and that animal," he said, pointing to his
30 eight-year-old golden retriever, Finn. "We walk all the
time and I take him to the park. You have to have
hobbies and you have to get your mind off work. People
who do well are able to deal with stress before it gets
too intense." The affable Finn is a fixture around
35 McNally's clinic and well known to the physician's
patients.

McNally, 47, has practiced for 18 years. He is happy that
his clinic escaped destruction from Hurricane Katrina
and that all four employees returned. Together they
40 were able to get the practice up and running quickly
after the storm. "I see a different spirit on the Coast.
People are working together," McNally said.
"My patients are much more appreciative of what we do
and there's more loyalty." He said he spends more time
45 with patients and much of that is dealing with social and
emotional issues of recovery. That makes it even more
important for him to maintain his exercise routine to
deal with his own stress.

Professional training creates expectations that we're
50 supposed to work hard to be successful and that mistakes
should not be made, says Phillip Hemphill, clinical
director of the Professional Enhancement Program at
Forrest General Hospital in Hattiesburg. "Professionals
often don't reach out for support," he said. "There's a lot
55 of competition out there and they feel they must be
perfect. These are some of the variables that create

stress." He says conquering stress is
an issue of boundaries and not
allowing work to spill over into other
60 parts of life. "People see that spillover
as normal and don't set boundaries.
That's partly because our identity is
tied up with our work," he said.
Hemphill advises rituals to separate
65 work and home life. It could be as
simple as changing clothes upon
arriving home or having a few
moments of silence to transition from
one part of life to another.

Source: Lofton, L. (2006, April 10).
Exercise, hobbies, small rituals can ease
stress. *Mississippi Business Journal.*

From the pages of

TIME

Lessons for Handling Stress

Diagnosing and dealing with stress

Take a deep breath. Now exhale slowly. You're probably not aware of it, but your heart has just slowed down. Not to worry; it will speed up again when you inhale.
5 This regular-irregular beat is a sign of a healthy interaction between heart and head. It's an ancient rhythm that helps your heart last a lifetime. And it leads to lesson No. 1 in how to manage stress
10 and avoid burnout.

NO. 1: REMEMBER TO BREATHE: Evolution has given to our brains a variety of mechanisms for handling the ups and downs of life, from built-in
15 chemical circuit breakers to entire networks of nerves whose only job is to calm you down. The problem is that they all require that you take regular breaks from your normal routine.

20 NO. 2: STRESS ALTERS YOUR BLOOD CHEMISTRY: For years psychologists have concentrated on the behavioral symptoms of burnout: lost energy, lost enthusiasm and lost
25 confidence. Now, thanks to new brain scans and more sophisticated blood tests, scientists can directly measure some of the effects of stress on mind and body, often with surprising results. You are
30 probably familiar with the signs of an adrenaline surge and you may have heard of cortisol, another stress hormone. But

did you know that too little cortisol in your bloodstream can be just as bad as too
35 much? Scientists know the most about cortisol because until now that has been the easiest part to measure. "But when one thing changes, all the others change to some degree," says Bruce McEwen, a
40 neuroendocrinologist at Rockefeller University. So just because you see an imbalance in one area doesn't mean you understand why it is happening.

NO. 3: YOU CAN'T AVOID STRESS:
45 Even getting out of bed can be tough on the body. Several hours before you wake each morning, a tiny region at the base of your cerebrum called the hypothalamus sends a signal that alerts your adrenal
50 glands to start pumping out cortisol, which acts as a wake-up signal. Cortisol levels continue to rise after you become conscious in what is sometimes referred to as the "Oh, s___! It's another day"
55 response. This may help explain why so many heart attacks and strokes occur between 6 a.m. and 8 a.m.

Most people's cortisol peaks a few hours after waking. Levels then gradually
60 decline during the day. That pattern

typically changes, however, in people who are severely depressed. Their cortisol level still rises early in the morning, but it stays high all day long. Researchers figured something similar had to be happening in burnout victims. But rather than finding a prominent cortisol peak, investigators discovered a shallow bump in the morning followed by a low, flattened level throughout the day.

NO. 4: STRESS CAN AGE YOU BEFORE YOUR TIME: Scientists have long suspected that unremitting stress does damage to the immune system, but they weren't sure how. Then two years ago, researchers at the University of California, San Francisco, looked at white blood cells from a group of mothers whose children suffered from chronic disorders like autism or cerebral palsy. The investigators found clear signs of accelerated aging in those study subjects who had cared the longest for children with disabilities or who reported the least control over their lives.

NO. 5: STRESS IS NOT AN EQUAL-OPPORTUNITY EMPLOYER: Researchers have found that subjects with low self-esteem are more vulnerable to stress. Jens Pruessner at McGill University in Montreal believes that the hippocampus, located deep in the brain, is at least partly responsible. The hippocampus is particularly sensitive to the amount of cortisol flooding your cerebrum, so when cortisol levels begin to rise, the hippocampus sends a set of signals that help shut down the cortisol cascade. Using several different types of brain scans, Pruessner has shown that people who test below average on self-esteem also tend to have smaller-than-average hippocampi.

NO. 6: THERE'S MORE THAN ONE WAY TO RELIEVE STRESS: This is probably the toughest lesson to internalize because when stress overwhelms the system, your choices often seem more limited than they are. Behavioral scientists have a name for this psychological reaction. They call it "learned helplessness", and they have studied the phenomenon closely in laboratory rodents. Obviously, humans have more intellectual resources at their disposal, but the underlying principle remains. When what used to work doesn't anymore, you lose your ability to reason. Just being aware of your nervous system's built-in bias toward learned helplessness in the face of unrelieved stress can help you identify and develop healthy habits that will buffer at least some of the load.

Transcripts

Unit 1: Communicating in Academic Situations

Track 1
Ex 2.3

Listen to another group of students reporting back on their discussion of the points in Ex 2.1. Which statements do they refer to?

1

Student A: Our group thought the most controversial point was the first one—wanting to speak English with a native-speaker accent.

2

Student B: Point "d," concerning the importance of grammar and pronunciation, provoked the most discussion in our group. Some people felt that grammar was more important than pronunciation, but others disagreed strongly.

3

Student A: Point "f" was the most controversial point of discussion in our group; people were very divided over the issue of working in groups affecting their grammatical accuracy.

4

Student B: There was some disagreement about point "g," the point about speaking English for social reasons, but most of the group agreed that international students will need to communicate socially.

Track 2
Ex 3.2

Listen to two students discussing these statements. Does the second speaker agree, disagree, or partly agree with each statement?

a)

Speaker A: If you want to succeed at the university, you really need to manage your time well.

Speaker B: Absolutely. I totally agree, because otherwise you will fall behind.

b)

Speaker A: It's important to do a lot of reading before you choose a focus for your essays.

Speaker B: Yes, that's true, but you need to limit the amount you read.

c)

Speaker A: The best time to review for exams is just before the exam, when the pressure is on.

Speaker B: I'm not sure I agree with you there. Many people can't think clearly under pressure.

d)

Speaker A: The same study skills are necessary for both undergraduate and postgraduate courses.

Speaker B: I agree up to a point, but graduates probably need more developed research skills.

e)

Speaker A: If you've completed an academic course in one country, you should be able to cope with a course in another country.

Speaker B:	Not necessarily. There are different academic cultures in different countries. You may have to learn a new approach to studying.
	f)
Speaker A:	People have different learning styles. It helps you learn more quickly if you're aware of how you learn best.
Speaker B:	That's a very good point. It can really help you to study more efficiently if you understand your own strengths and weaknesses.

Track 3
Ex 4.1

Listen and number the points below according to the order in which the students discuss them.

Sarah:	Hi Majid, how are you doing?
Majid:	Yes, I am fine, and you Sarah?
Sarah:	I'm fine, I haven't seen you in ages. How is your course work going now?
Majid:	It's just too much, to be honest. Too much.
Sarah:	Are you really busy?
Majid:	Yes, really, really busy.
Sarah:	I'm in my final year now and I have an awful lot of work to do. I'm studying history and there's so much reading.
Majid:	Yes, it's the same with me, you know. I am studying Applied Linguistics and I'm just in over my head. There's so much reading.
Sarah:	How do you cope with all the reading?
Majid:	I try just to prioritize my reading lists. This is what I do. I read on a daily basis—I'm not sure—as a native speaker maybe that's not your technique, is it?
Sarah:	Well, being a native-speaking student, I try to leave my reading to the last minute. But how do you pick out the relevant things in your reading list? As a history student, I get a list as long as my arm of different books to read by different people, and sometimes you don't know what's important. How do you do that?
Majid:	I just try to focus on my lecture and after the class I ask my instructor which book would be very easy to read and give me an introduction about the topic. Otherwise I would just end up wasting my time searching for books that are relevant.
Sarah:	Same here. I always try to speak to my instructors and ask them which book is the best to read. And also, because I'm studying a subject where I have to write a lot of essays and a lot of analytical writing, I also try to ask them about who is on which side of the debate and who would give the best answer to a question.
Majid:	Yes, that's a very good idea. Do you mean that you try to ask your instructor about which book or what kind of writer each writer is, I mean try to understand the argument first?
Sarah:	In my courses, there's an awful lot about different theories and different approaches to events that happened in the past and so it's very important when I look at my reading list to be able to see who said what about an event. So that helps a lot. But it still takes an awful lot of time.

Majid:	Yes, and how do you manage your time?
Sarah:	You go first.
Majid:	I have to be honest because the reading is very difficult. I try to finish an article very quickly and follow the techniques that we learned in the ESL course, for example like skimming and scanning, and read the abstract first, things like this. And that's just to help me to cope with the time.
Sarah:	I wish that they'd taught us all these little handy hints and tips. As a native-speaking student they just expect you to know what to do.
Majid:	Hmm!
Sarah:	And, with, you know, trying to manage your time as well as all this reading, you've got all these essays and presentations to do throughout the semester and sometimes you feel that you've got so much going on, there's an awful lot of stress. How do you manage stress?
Majid:	It's very difficult, a killer to be honest, and sometimes I just leave it and just have a chat with a friend or just relax sometimes, you know?
Sarah:	Over the length of a semester, generally things aren't very consistent. Some weeks you may have presentations and essays to do and some weeks you may only have a little reading. I find it helps to manage your time by, say, doing something before you have to do it, doing reading before you have to do it and also essays as well. Do you find that doing an essay early helps?
Majid:	Yes, that's what I do. I start very early. I make a kind of a plan before I start my essay and then send it to my instructor and I ask if it's a good plan or not and if I can start writing on that topic if the plan is okay. And they usually give you very good feedback, and after the feedback I start reading and writing and try to finish very early. And when you finish your essays, how do you edit them, what kinds of things do you do to them?
Sarah:	When I write an essay, I try to write it in parts, but I don't know if this is a very good technique, it's just what I've done for many years. Once I've finished an essay, I read it and then I get someone else to read it, to make sure it makes sense and that it's not just made-up stuff in my head that doesn't make any sense at all. It's very important to have someone else read your work before you hand it in. Because especially in extended writing, where it's your thoughts going down on paper, it's very important that it makes sense.
Majid:	Do you choose the topic that you are going to write about?
Sarah:	Yes, it's very important when you choose any course that you're interested in it and want to take it. It must be even more important as a non-native speaker to be interested in what you're doing, so that you have the drive to keep going and persevere when things are hard.

Track 4
Ex 6.1

Now listen to a student presenting his top five study tips. Are any of the points the same as yours?

Student:	There are five main points which we consider important for studying successfully.
	Our first point is you need to be well-organized. Without this, you will not be able to manage all the work you are given.

Next is the importance of working with classmates. Students often need to cooperate with each other in classes and planning presentations.

Moving on to our third point, keep good notes. There is so much information to deal with from both classes and reading that you need to take notes effectively and reread these.

Fourth, we think that good IT skills are now an essential part of university study. Students often need to use the Internet for research purposes, so they need to know how to search for useful information.

And finally, our last point is the importance of motivation—you really need to *want* to learn about your subject. If not, you'll find it hard to study if you're just not interested in it.

Unit 2: Classes and Discussions

Track 5
Ex 2.3

Now listen to a student comparing different perspectives on the statement in Ex 2.1. What does the speaker say about the views of those involved?

Student: From a teacher's perspective, he or she would probably be concerned about the effect of the child's behavior on other children—how it might negatively affect their progress and learning—so the teacher would probably want the child excluded from school.

From the point of view of the parents, they would say it was the instructor's and school's responsibility to deal with the child's behavior problems and that excluding the child was an easy way out for the school. They would say that the child should remain and the school should work out a solution.

If I were the principal of the child's school, I'd probably feel that the reputation of the school might be damaged by excluding the child. It might give the school a bad name because people might think it was a problem school. As a principal, I'd want the child to remain at the school, despite the problems.

The child psychologist would argue that we need to understand and deal with the cause of the child's bad behavior, and that excluding the child would not do that. In fact, it might damage the child more.

Track 6
Ex 4.1

Listen to a student summarizing a group discussion of the statement from Ex 2.1 relating to the exclusion of disruptive children. Did the group agree or disagree with the statement?

Student: This is a difficult question, but we finally all agreed that such a child should be excluded from school, because this would be in the best interests of most people concerned. It's true that this action might cause some damage to the child's long-term ability to socialize effectively with other children, so we also agreed that this action should only be taken if there is no other solution, I mean, if all else fails.

Track 7
Ex 4.4

Listen to a student using some of the phrases.

Student:
After much consideration, we decided that corporal punishment is not really necessary to maintain discipline in schools.

All things considered, we felt that children should not leave school until they are 18.

On balance, we felt that parents should not be allowed to educate their children at home.

We couldn't reach agreement on this issue. Some of us felt that corporal punishment is necessary, whilst others disagreed strongly.

We recognized that there are some disadvantages for the child, such as pressure and stress, but we still felt tests at a young age are a good idea.

We're fully aware that lack of discipline in schools is a major problem. However, we still felt that corporal punishment is not the answer.

We have to acknowledge that some parents could educate their children very well. We still felt, however, that only parents with teaching qualifications should be allowed to do this by law.

So, although we agreed with the statement, we stressed that 15-year-olds should get careful counselling on which subjects to choose.

Unit 3: Examining Underlying Assumptions

Track 8
Ex 3.3

Listen to a student presenting key points from the same article.

Student:
As the title suggests, this article deals with an apparent change in the role men would like to play in family life. First of all, it looks at the way fathers take a different attitude to mothers. It highlights the fact that the mother's role has developed over many years, but that the role fathers play has yet to be established.

The article quotes from a psychologist from the University of Texas-Austin, who says that it's now becoming the norm for fathers to be involved in bringing up their children. The reason for the change is largely due to the fact women want more equality in taking responsibility in the home.

Another psychologist at San Francisco State University sees the current group of fathers as a pilot group who are working out how to deal with the new situation facing them. He feels that they don't worry too much about being judged, as expectations are not high.

Finally, a psychiatrist from Yale University talks about the change in student population over the last twenty-five years in courses in child development. He points out that it's not unusual these days to have all male students in such courses.

So, the article reports on some interesting changes in social attitudes to work and fatherhood. However, it doesn't mention the effect of socioeconomic background on men's decisions or wishes regarding work and parenthood. I mean, the men who are choosing or wanting to give up work to become househusbands, are these men from high, middle, or lower income groups? We don't know this from the text, but this could be significant data.

Listen to the three extracts and underline where the speaker slows down and stresses particular words or phrases.

Extract 1

Student: The article also gives statistics from a magazine survey of 2,000 couples in the UK. As you can see, only one-third of those asked, 34 per cent in fact, wanted to continue working full-time after having children. The majority either wanted to return to part-time work or become full-time househusbands.

Extract 2

Student: The article then goes on to say that the social stigma attached to men stopping work to bring up a family is disappearing … social stigma—this means something people might be ashamed of doing, that society would not approve of. As I said, this is disappearing in the US as well, so you now see more men coming to schools and playgroups to pick up their children.

Extract 3

Student: So, the article reports on some interesting changes in social attitudes to work and fatherhood in the UK. However, it doesn't mention the effect of socioeconomic background on men's decisions or wishes regarding work and parenthood. I mean, the men who are choosing or wanting to give up work to become househusbands, are these men from high, middle or lower income groups?

Track 10
Ex 5.4

Listen to some students exchanging opinions on different topics. Check the expressions you hear.

1

Student A: It seems to me that women are being forced to have careers when they really want to stay at home.

Student B: I take your point, but don't you think that's making an assumption that all women want to have children?

2

Student A: In my view, women are biologically designed to bring up children, and men to be the breadwinners.

Student B: Well, I think that's a pretty old-fashioned idea.

3

Student A: Just because it's traditional or normal for women to stay at home, that doesn't necessarily mean it's natural.

Student B: I understand what you're saying, but you have to consider this question from the perspective of different cultures.

4

Student A: Women are built differently and aren't suitable for certain jobs, such as engineering and construction.

Student B: Well, I'm not sure if that's quite true—you need to consider the reality, that in fact a number of women are employed in the construction industry.

Unit 4: Reading into Speaking

Track 11
Ex 4.2

Listen to some of these expressions in context. Check the ones that you hear.

1

Student A: It's not really up to the government to do something about smoking, is it? Why do we always expect the government to deal with these kinds of issues, rather than making smokers themselves face up to the problem?

Student B: So what you're saying is that there's no point in the government trying to tackle the problem of smoking until individuals take responsibility for their own health …

2

Student A: I don't see why this subject gets so much attention. People have always had to work hard, and I'm sure it'll continue like that. If you're organized, it shouldn't be a problem.

Student B: So in your view, dealing with stress isn't a major issue; people just need to manage their time properly …

3

Student A: As far as I am concerned, it needs to be approached from the perspective of having a healthy and happy lifestyle … do you understand what I mean?

Student B: Yes, absolutely.

4

Student A: The fast food industry is only concerned with making a profit. It will mislead the public about what's in the junk food they sell. It can't be left to police itself.

Student B: I'm not sure I understand what you mean.

Student A: What I'm saying is that the fast food industry isn't concerned about people's health. They just want to make money, so they won't tell the truth about what they put in hamburgers, for example. The government needs to pass laws controlling what can be put in junk food. You can't just leave it to the fast food industry to decide.

Unit 5: The Use of Data

Track 12
Ex 3.2

Listen to the description of the data shown and answer the following questions.

Speaker: The graph shows movie admissions per age group between 2003 and 2007.

As you can see, young people aged between 15 and 24 are the most likely age group to go to the movies. There were 48 million admissions from this age group in the US in 2007. In 2007, there were 34 million admissions from the next most frequent age group, as can be seen from this line here. The overall admissions across all age groups have risen slightly.

From this data, it's clear that going to the movies is still a popular form of entertainment, despite the arrival of videos, DVDs, and computer games.

Track 13
Ex 4.1

You are going to hear a journalist talking about the British Broadcasting Corporation (BBC).

Interviewer: So Paul, can you tell us a little bit about how the BBC got started initially?

BBC employee: The BBC was set up in 1922. Um, its first director general was a 33-year-old Scottish engineer called John Reith, who was invited to become the first director and his vision, it is important to know this guy's name, John Reith, his vision was very important for the establishing of the BBC. His vision of what it should be was very, very influential. Um, basically he had a phrase which he used which was to inform, educate, and entertain. And these were the three pillars of what he thought the BBC should do.

Interviewer: Mmm.

BBC employee: Inform, educate, and entertain, in that order. It is interesting that educate comes before entertain.

Interviewer: I see.

BBC employee: Yes, in his vision of it, and this kind of motto is still used in the BBC today, inform, educate, and entertain, and it can still be seen in something that is called the Reith Lectures that take place every year. Radio lectures on an important scientific or cultural issue of the day which are dedicated to Lord Reith, the first director general.

Interviewer: And was it accepted from very early on that the BBC would be an independent organization editorially?

BBC employee: Yes, um, that is very interesting, um, John Reith's vision was that the BBC should be financially independent and editorially independent. Financially, well he had seen the commercial radio being set up in the US and commercial radio was basically paid for by the advertising. So the advertisers had a lot of power, and he had seen other European broadcasters being set up, who were controled by the government, and so there was a lot of political influence over them. And he wanted something that would be completely separate from both of them, and that was his vision.

He was tested very early on, actually, in 1926, only four years after the BBC was set up there was the General Strike. This took place during the Great Depression of the '20s and everybody was on strike. Newspapers weren't being printed, people couldn't get information and the Home Secretary at the time, Mr. Winston Churchill, tried to use the BBC to broadcast government propaganda. But John Reith was very, very strict about this, absolutely refused to broadcast what he saw as government propaganda and tried to broadcast independently what the BBC thought was actually happening, and I guess this was the beginning of the BBC's reputation for total independence in its news reporting.

Interviewer: Yes, I mean one of the most admirable qualities of the BBC has been its ability to maintain its independence and, um, I'm wondering if this has been challenged in various, if it's still being challenged over this.

BBC employee: The BBC's political independence has been challenged constantly over its history, really. Especially in the last twenty years, it has been attacked by both right-wing and left-wing political parties. In the 1980s, Margaret Thatcher and the Conservative Party used to call it the Bolshevik Broadcasting Company. Bolshevik as in the Russian Revolution, they claimed it was very biased and left-wing. And in 2003, the left-wing party, the Labour Party, had a very serious falling out with the BBC over the Iraq war. What became known as the Kelly Affair. Basically the BBC claimed in a radio program that the government had deliberately exaggerated the threat from Saddam Hussein's Iraq in order to persuade the public to go to war with Iraq. The government denied that they had been misleading the public. They were very angry about the BBC's report and the scientist at the center of this big argument, who had actually given the information to the BBC, unfortunately committed suicide, and there was a great big argument, big public investigation about this, and in the end the judge who was leading the investigation, decided for the government and against the BBC, and the BBC had to apologize and the leader, actually the director general at the time actually, resigned, although a lot of the general public didn't agree with this ruling.

Interviewer: Absolutely, yes.

BBC employee: It was a very serious setback for the BBC.

Interviewer: Yes, and it was very evident in the march to London when one million people took to the streets to demonstrate against the government.

BBC employee: Certainly, yeah, and that had to be reported just by the BBC just as much as the propaganda for going to war with Iraq was reported, and they both had to be reported in a balanced way.

Interviewer: Yes, so in many ways the BBC has been a very controversial organization throughout the ages since it started.

BBC employee: It certainly has.

Interviewer: I am wondering how it manages to finance itself throughout all of this.

BBC employee: Well, the BBC has a special, I think unique, form of financing at the moment, where it gets money from people, from everybody who has a TV. If you have a TV in your house you must pay a license for it every year, and that includes students. That might be some of your students might need to get one. The licenses are £139.50, I think, and …

Interviewer: Quite a substantial amount!

BBC Employee: Quite a substantial amount, which you have to pay every year and this money is used for making radio and TV programs. The BBC has other ways of making money and it sells its programs abroad to other channels, it makes books which tie in with its programs and it has various merchandizing branches, but it doesn't carry advertising. The only advertising you will see on the BBC is for other BBC programs.

Interviewer: Yes, yes. And it is one of the reasons why people opt to watch BBC rather than other channels.

BBC employee: Some people find it very refreshing not to have to have advertisements on every 15 minutes.

Interviewer: Yes, especially in the middle of films.

And the BBC still does continue to play a very important role in people's lives. Very often at lunchtime, breaktime, you'll hear people talking about a program that they had seen on television.

BBC employee: Yes, the BBC plays an integral part in British life. People have grown up with it for generations. There are soap operas on BBC radio which are 50 years old. It is the oldest soap opera in the world. It is the nation's favourite information source. Most people still get their information from the BBC. The BBC is still the most trusted organization in the country.

Interviewer: So why do you think the BBC still plays such an important role in British life? I mean, very often at lunchtime, the topic of conversation would be a program that people have watched the night before.

BBC employee: Absolutely, I think the BBC still plays an integral part in British life. People have grown up with it for generations. It is like a trusted friend. It is still where people get most of their information from. Certainly, the BBC is more trusted than any politician and people are very protective of it. They don't like to see the BBC being attacked by politicians. I also think people are very proud of the BBC. They see broadcasting as something that we still do well in this country. The BBC itself still claims that it has the second most recognized brand name in the world.

Interviewer: And it certainly offers us a lot. Thank you very much, Paul.

BBC employee: Thank you

Interviewer: Very informative.

Track 14
Ex 5.3

Listen to three students discussing freedom of speech and answer the following questions.

Student A: I don't think you can really put any limits on freedom of speech. It should be an absolute principle in a mature democracy, don't you think?

Student B: When you say "an absolute principle," do you mean that anyone can say or broadcast or print anything they want to about anyone else on any subject?

Student A: Yes, I think so. Obviously, you expect that people will use that right responsibly and not use it in a way that will lead to violence, or worse.

Student C: Yes, I think I agree. I mean, once you start putting limits on freedom of speech, then it's a dangerous road to go down. As you said, it's a fundamental part of a democratic society. If those in authority start restricting that right, if those in power have the right to decide what can or can't be said, then I think it's a dangerous sort of power to have. You made an interesting point about using the right to freedom of speech in a responsible way. That's what I think a mature democracy should be based on—people have the right to free speech, but are responsible enough not to abuse it, not to exercise it in a negative way.

Student B: Yes, but following on from that point, that's where I have a problem with the idea of an absolute right to freedom of speech, particularly regarding what you both say about responsibility and mature democracies. The reality is people can't be trusted to use that right in a responsible way. Why should people have the right to make racist comments or things which might cause violence against others, or whatever? Can I also pick up on your point about not allowing those in power to limit freedom of speech? I mean, I would have thought that in a mature democracy, yes, those in power must listen to the majority, but they also need to protect minorities, and that means limiting the rights of people to say things in public which might put those minority groups in danger.

Student A: OK, those are fair arguments, but you make the point that a society needs to protect minority groups, but if the government can limit freedom of speech, they might start silencing minority groups and that's not protecting them. There might be less tolerance of different, non-majority views and opinions.

Student C: Exactly.

Student B: I know, it's not an easy question, but I still think that a society in which anyone can say anything may in fact lead to a less tolerant society than one where there are some limits on what you can say. As I said before, people might use free speech to take away the freedom of other people to feel safe in a society.

Student C: I think we'll have to agree to disagree on this issue.

Unit 7: Supporting Your Point of View

Track 15
Ex 4.4

Listen to the interview.

Interviewer: Good morning, Sonia. You've done some research into the role of women in the construction industry specifically. Can I start, however, by asking you about the participation of women in the labor market more generally? What are the reasons why more women are participating in the labor market?

Sonia Gurjao: The main reasons for women's increased participation in the labor market would be the deskilling of historically male jobs. Secondly, demographics have changed. We have an increased life expectancy and women today tend to have fewer children than they did in the past. We also have a restructuring of psychological expectations, such as women's own expectations of themselves and what they want to do in life and today, in today's day and age, it's become an economic necessity to have two incomes in a family to be able to support a family and to be able to accommodate the general running of the house.

Interviewer: Is that because of the cost of living?

Sonia Gurjao: Yes, that is because of the increased cost of living today. And another reason is women are more highly educated today than they have ever been in the past. And all these factors contribute towards their increased participation in the labor market.

Interviewer: Now, moving on to the construction industry itself. Is the construction industry a common career choice for women?

Sonia Gurjao: No, actually, the construction industry is not an obvious career choice for women. In fact, lots of women are not informed about the construction industry as a career of choice. This starts right from schools, where they aren't informed of construction, science, engineering, and technology subjects as a choice that they could take or pursue as their career choices. And one of the reasons is the construction industry also has a bad image, that is one related to hard work, and working in extreme conditions. It's known as the dirty industry and it's not attractive to women as such.

Interviewer: As I understand it, from your research, the construction industry does need more women though to join it? Why is that?

Sonia Gurjao: The construction industry plays a critical role in Britain's prosperity and it employs over two million people, and in the past it had a steady choice of entrants into the industry, probably because of the way people chose their careers and people pursued vocational training, but with the change in the education system and people pursuing higher education, the traditional source of labor doesn't tend to go into vocational training and so we now see a skills shortage in the construction industry. And with 50 per cent of the labor participation being women, today for the construction industry, including women within construction becomes a very important aspect.

Interviewer: Has the construction industry itself made any attempts to try to recruit women into the industry?

Sonia Gurjao: The construction industry has not actively gone into recruiting women, but as they've seen, and as the government's seen that there's going to be a problem with recruiting your traditional force of labor, they've started looking into recruiting women as a solution to the labor problems and also making the construction industry more inclusive and looking for talent from the other 50 per cent of the labor workforce. So, what they've done is they've gone to schools and they have projects where they encourage young girls to do, like they have little training sessions and they have workshops where they actively participate and build things to encourage them or to show them what working in the construction industry might be like.

Interviewer: So, they've gone to the schools …

Sonia Gurjao: They've started from school and then they have, even for young people, they've started for career advisors, they've started training career advisors into encouraging or to stop stereotyping career choices for young people.

Interviewer: And that's to try and encourage young girls …

Sonia Gurjao: Not just young girls, but also encourage boys as well into construction. Because it's not only girls who lack interest in the construction industry, it's also the lack of men in the construction industry.

Interviewer: I understand that the industry has a problem with keeping women who join the construction industry. Why is that and is there a solution to this problem?

Sonia Gurjao: I think that's a recent realization from the part of the industry. They have a long-working-hour culture because of the kind of projects there are, because they tend to be projects that need to have deadlines, because of the cost involved in the projects as well. So, ultimately what happens is when you have women who are 50 per cent of the workforce, but then out of these 50 per cent of the workforce, around 44 per cent of women actually only work part-time and the industry doesn't have part-time working, so that makes it difficult for women to have a presence in the industry, to be working. So that's where the industry has started realizing that if we have to recruit women we have to make an attempt to be flexible, as in other industries like telecommunications and banking, which have of course benefited from making their jobs flexible.

Interviewer: Could you just summarize what you see to be the main barriers which women face today in joining or staying in the construction industry?

Sonia Gurjao: What we've repeatedly heard in the past is that the construction industry is dirty, dangerous and not suitable for women. But in today's day and age, where technology has taken over and we have more managing of projects and we have consultancy, so in today's construction industry, the main barriers would actually be flexible working in terms of 44 per cent of women actually working part-time in the labor force participation. If we need to target that, we need to make the industry more flexible and it needs to see that people need to have a better work/life balance and organizations need to change to accommodate this.

Unit 8: Collecting and Presenting Data

Track 16
Ex 4.2

Listen to a student using *Useful language* expressions from Ex 1.5. Underline the words or phrases in the box that the speaker uses.

1   Most of the respondents claimed that they take recycling seriously and recycled glass, plastic, and paper products.

2   Approximately a third of those interviewed were prepared to be part of a car-pooling plan.

3   Just over 50 per cent of the subjects said that they would buy environmentally-friendly products even if those products were more expensive.

Unit 10: The Importance of Reflection

Track 17
Ex 3.1

Listen to a speaker who recently completed a degree at an American university.

Text 1

EAP instructor: Hello, Gulin. Thanks for agreeing to come and talk about the experience of studying here as an international student. You're just finishing a one-year Master's degree course, aren't you?

Gulin: Yes, that's right.

EAP instructor: What has it been like for you, working with American and other international students together?

Gulin: Well, it has been a new kind of experience for me. Everything was new to me at the beginning. But as in any new situation, I gradually learned to adapt. I think that, if you're studying at a university with people from all over the world, then you need to accept that there will be cultural differences between people and you need to be tolerant of them so that you can get along with people well enough to work with them. Oh, and of course, it's right to expect other people to show a similar acceptance and tolerance towards you.

EAP instructor: Yes, I know that students are sometimes advised to form study groups with others on the course. Did you do that, and, if so, was it helpful?

Gulin: Yes, I agree that it's a good idea. But of course it doesn't work with just anybody. I think it's worth looking for people who have similar study habits to your own, and if possible people who don't live too far away from you. And, again, you have to be prepared to be flexible; to adjust your own approach a little sometimes, so that it's easier for the other people to work with you.

EAP instructor: Now, what about the professor? When you started your course, was it clear to you how to approach the professor and what for?

Gulin: I think the responsibilities of the professor are written in the department's handbook.

EAP instructor: That's good.

Gulin: So the student should read that to get a basic idea of the support she is entitled to expect from her professor. But you need to play it by ear a little at first, because obviously professors are human and so they're different. You have to approach different professors in different ways. One point I would make about meetings with your professor is: it is worth preparing a little bit before the meeting—working out the questions you want to ask and the kind of answers you expect or need, so that you make the best possible use of the time during the meeting. Personally, I take in a list of points in order of priority: like 1, 2, 3, 4, etc.

EAP instructor: Apart from your professor and fellow students, what other resources have you made use of during your period of study?

Gulin: Well, I would advise any new student to explore the university campus thoroughly early on in her stay, if possible with some guidance from a more experienced student to get to know the facilities that are available. The first place I explored was the library—it is important to find which parts of the library are particularly relevant to your subject area, and to discover whether there are other, specialist libraries or collections in some departments. For example, in my case, there were books on linguistics in one part of the main library, periodicals in the other part, and then there was the departmental library and also a useful library in a neighboring college. It took a while to discover where everything was.

But the library is not the only facility which is open to all students from all departments: some departments or units run an advisory service. This means that at certain times of the day students from any department can go along and ask for help with their project. It's well worthwhile asking about these advisory services early on in your course, and don't be afraid to make use of them—they are there to help students, that's their function.

EAP instructor: Did you use these advisory services yourself?

Gulin: Oh, yes, two of them. The technician in the Computer Lab has helped me several times: once when my computer crashed, and another time when I thought I'd lost a lot of data … And the Applied Statistics Department also runs an advisory service, which I would recommend to anyone who's going to do experimental research. The staff there will discuss the design of your experiment with you—of course, you should do this early on in your paper at the planning stage, so that it's not too late to make any changes that they suggest. They will also help you to analyze the data later on.

EAP instructor: Right. The facilities you've mentioned so far have been broadly academic. What other kinds would you advise new students to make use of?

Gulin: They should make use of the Student Union, of course; after all, it's supposed to be run by the students for the students.

EAP instructor: I imagine those organizations are a good way for international students to meet American students, for social reasons and also perhaps to practice speaking English.

Gulin: Yeah, I agree.

EAP instructor: Did you do that yourself? Did you join one of these clubs?

Gulin: Oh yeah, I joined the Chess Club. That was a good move, because sometimes you need a place where you can take a break from your academic studies for a while. Chess is always refreshing; you sit down and … I guess you use a different part of the brain. And as well as the chess itself, there is the social contact. People tend to talk a lot at our chess evenings; maybe not so much during, but before and after their games; not just about chess—all kinds of things.

EAP instructor: And what about sports? I know there are a lot of sports clubs advertised on the notice boards as well.

Gulin: Yeah, there are various sports, and the one I'm interested in is mountaineering …

EAP instructor: Mountaineering!

Gulin: Yeah. It can be quite demanding, but it gives you a sense of satisfaction when you climb … the highest mountain in the state, for example.

EAP instructor: I'll have to take your word for that. Right, finally, is there any advice that you wish you'd had at the beginning of your studies here?

Gulin: Yes, to be prepared for a style of lecture in which contributions from the audience are often invited by the professor. If you are not used to this style, it can at first seem off-putting, even aggressive. Try to practice contributing so that you can join in the discussion.

Perhaps I should explain that, although contributions to the class discussion were encouraged, it was certainly not acceptable for a student to engage in private discussion with the one or two people nearest to him during a lecture. That happened a couple of times in the first week of my course, and it was an irritating distraction for the professor and all the other students.

One final point: make an effort to see the major as a whole from the start. If, as in my case, the most important part of the degree in terms of both assessment and learning is a dissertation, start thinking about this from the beginning of your course work. Jot down ideas about it from time to time, to help you gradually work towards it.

EAP instructor: Well, thank you very much, Gulin. You've been very helpful.

Gulin: It was a pleasure.

Track 18
Ex 3.1

Listen to a speaker who recently completed a degree at an American university.

Text 2

EAP instructor: Now, Chris, can I get this right? You've just completed a Master's degree and a large proportion of the students in your classes were international students? Is that right?

Chris: That's correct. Yes, I was in AERD—that's the Department of Agricultural Extension and Rural Development.

EAP instructor: And how do you think the students from other countries did with that major?

Chris: Pretty well. I think we found as the classes went on that we were all in the same boat. For example, the majority of both American and international students were returning to full-time study after several years in work. That was an important thing to have in common.

EAP instructor: What advice would you give students, particularly international students, based on your experience as a student here?

Chris: I think the most basic thing is to make use, full use, of your advisors and professors. Maybe some of the international students, perhaps even some of the American students, don't do that. They're a little too shy in the beginning to take questions or problems to professors or to make use of the time that professors make available. So, the first piece of advice I'd give, I think, is to find out at the beginning of the semester the times at which your professor is going to be available for office hours, and then make full use of them.

EAP instructor: So, any problems, they should tell the professor as soon as possible?

Chris: Yes.

EAP instructor: Moving on, what about the amount of reading that you have to do as a student?

Chris: Yes! It looked pretty daunting at first, with those long reading lists. I think the important point here is to be selective: don't think you have to read everything that's listed—you're not expected to. Find which are the most important items on the list—ask the professor if necessary, and then, if your time is limited, spend it reading those books thoroughly.

EAP instructor: What about study resources on the campus—the library, for example. Any tips there?

Chris: Yes, make use of the recall system. If, when you get to the library, you find that the particular books you need have been borrowed by someone else, don't give up. Fill out a recall slip, hand it in at the information desk, and within a few days the library will contact you to tell you the book is now ready to pick up. Once I discovered this system, unfortunately not until halfway through my course, I used it a lot and I found it very helpful. Of course, it means you need to plan your work properly; don't leave the essential reading for an assignment until just before the deadline, and then try to use the recall system—it's too late then.

EAP instructor: Any advice on working with other students?

Chris: When you are given an assignment, definitely talk to your fellow students about it: discuss your initial ideas about it, and then later how you're doing with it, what you're finding difficult, etc. This will help you to think around the topic, and also reassure you that you are not the only person feeling the strain.

And if you want, you can try setting up a study group with some of the others. In our major, for example, five of us formed a study group in the second semester and worked together on reviewing for the exams. But a study group can be helpful at any point in the course—for a particular assignment, for instance. You need to work out which of the other students in your courses you find it easy to work with, maybe people who have the same approach to study as you, or simply people who live in the same residence hall as you. I got together with four others and we decided that we could do the reading for the exams more enjoyably and more efficiently by sharing it. So we agreed which person should read which item on the list, and then we met up once or twice a week after classes and summarized our reading for each other. And when someone wasn't clear about something, or disagreed with something, we discussed it. I learned a lot from that. It also made me more confident about expressing my ideas, as you need to do in seminars.

EAP instructor: So, try to form a study group with other students to share the workload.

Chris: Yes.

EAP instructor: Now, what about choosing classes? That's often a very important part of your course of study, making selections about exactly what you will study. Any advice?

Chris: One point I would make is, perhaps it's obvious: choose classes according to which subject interests you, not according to who the professor is. Don't choose a class simply because it's organized by someone who gives nice, clear lectures. There may be a greater risk of some overseas students making this mistake because they are so concerned about understanding every word of a lecture. But we all agreed, at the end of our studies, that the subject, not the professor, should be the most important consideration when you choose classes. If you choose a subject that really interests you, it's likely to provide you with a dissertation topic that you are really motivated to work on.

EAP instructor: Right, well that's …

Chris: So, go for the subject not the professor.

EAP instructor: That's my next question, actually! Any advice on writing the thesis or dissertation?

Chris: As soon as you have drafted a proposal, an outline of what you intend to write about, have a meeting with your professor or supervisor to establish whether the basic idea is viable. This is important because otherwise you might spend a lot of time working on a project, only to discover at a later stage that a supervisor has some basic objection to what you're doing, and you have wasted a lot of time. So, have an early meeting to get some official feedback on your proposal.

One other point about working on a major project, such as a dissertation: draw up a work schedule at the beginning, with reasonable deadlines by which you intend to complete each stage of the project. The project can seem like a huge mountain to climb at first, so it's good for morale if you divide it up into manageable sections: "I'll finish reading by the end of April, I'll complete data collection by mid-May, and then I'll write the first two chapters by the end of May"; that kind of thing. Even if you don't meet all the deadlines, you will have a sense of progress.

EAP instructor: OK, that's very helpful, Chris. Thank you very much.

Chris: Not at all.

Appendix 1: Signpost Expressions for Presentations

Introducing the presentation

Good morning/afternoon, ladies and gentlemen …

The topic of my presentation today is …

Today I am going to talk about …

If you have any questions, I would be happy to answer these at the end of the presentation.

Giving an overview of the presentation

This presentation will deal with three main points …

My presentation is divided into three main sections …

First of all I will … then I will move on to examine … and finally …

Transition expressions

Moving on to the next point, …

Now I'd like to look at …

The third area which needs to be considered is …

And finally, my last point is …

Referring to visual aids

As you can see …

From this chart/table/graph, it is clear that …

This graph/table/chart shows …

Concluding the presentation

Finally, …

To sum up, …

As this presentation has clearly shown, it is essential that …

Thank you for your attention … are there any questions?

Appendix 2: Table

Statements	Different perspectives			
1 Corporal punishment is necessary to maintain discipline.	Instructors: Many would support this as the only way to control large classes.			
2 Children should be given formal tests and exams from the age of six.				
3 Children should be allowed to leave school at 16 if they wish.				
4 Parents should be allowed to educate children at home if they wish.				
5 Children should be able to choose which subjects they want to study at the age of 15.				

New "Daditude": Today's fathers are hands-on

Change in the role of men in family life. Fathers also taking different attitude to mothers.

Now becoming the norm for fathers to be involved in bringing up their children as women want more equality in taking responsibility in the home.

Mother's role developed over many years, but role fathers play not yet established.

Current group of fathers seen as a pilot group – they are still working out how to deal with the new situation facing them. Tend not to worry too much about being judged, as expectations are not high.

Many men now training for their role with proportion of male students on child development courses increasing. These days not unusual to have all male students on such courses.

OHT 2

New "Daditude": Today's fathers are hands-on

Fathers involved in bringing up their children now becoming norm

- women want more equality in the home.

(Research at University of Texas-Austen)

Fathers taking different attitude to mothers

- mothers' role developed over decades; fathers' role not yet established.

- current group of fathers seen as a pilot–still working out how to deal with the new situation.

- tendency not to worry about being judged, as expectations are not high.

(Research at San Francisco State University)

Increase in men on child development courses

- not unusual to have all male students on such courses.

Appendix 4: Preparing and Planning a Presentation

There are many aspects of a good presentation and, during the course, you have worked on some of these aspects.

In some cases, you were giving a short presentation about a topic in order to lead into a discussion. In other cases, you were presenting information, a summary of a text, or a program. However, in future situations you may be giving a presentation based on your own work or research, and you will need to spend a lot of time working on the content and organization of the presentation. Below is a list of stages you may find helpful.

Stage 1: Find out what you need to do

1 Make sure you know exactly what the topic is or, if you are choosing your own topic, what is expected of you.

2 Check the length of time you have for the presentation.

3 Think about your audience—how much are they likely to know about the topic/how much will you need to explain?

4 If the presentation is being assessed, make sure you know what the criteria are.

Stage 2: Brainstorm ideas

5 Make a list of anything you can think of related to your topic; you will not use all of these ideas, but will choose from them afterwards.

6 Look at your list of ideas—what connections can you see between them? Are there particular ideas you could develop that would be of interest to your audience?

7 Decide which ideas to use—can each one be summarized in one sentence? If not, perhaps your ideas are not clear and specific enough.

8 Explain your ideas to a friend—this will help you to clarify them.

Stage 3: Do any necessary research

9 Determine if there are any ideas you need to get more information about.

10 Gather any evidence you need to support your ideas, e.g., statistics.

11 Think about how much information you can realistically convey to your audience.

12 Keep your audience in mind, especially in relation to their level of expertise.

Stage 4: Organize your ideas

13 Decide which point you should begin with.

14 Think about how you can link one idea to the next.

15 Do not include too much information—you want your audience to understand your key points clearly.

16 Decide how you will begin and end your presentation. In the introduction you want to get the attention of the audience. The conclusion is the last part of your presentation, and probably what the audience will most remember.

17 Prepare your PowerPoint slides—remember: "less is more."

18 Think of the key words you will use and check your pronunciation with a native speaker—there is nothing worse than listening to a presentation where the presenter pronounces the title of the presentation incorrectly!

Stage 5: **Practice …**

19 to make sure you know your content well.

20 to check the time of the presentation.

22 to develop your confidence.

23 to anticipate some of the questions people might ask.

24 to make sure that your presentation does justice to all the hard work you have put into preparing it.

Appendix 5: Possible Topics for Class Discussions

Congestion charging is the most effective means of preventing traffic congestion.

Banning smoking in public places contravenes human rights.

Women should play the same role as men in the armed forces.

Free education is an impractical dream.

People should not be allowed to ...

GM food is the best means of solving global shortages.

Globalization is only a threat to a small minority of individual cultures.

Sports should play a far greater role in school curricula.

The advance of information technology is creating a less sociable society.

The development of free markets is the most effective way of solving the world's economic problems.

Appendix 6: Career Drivers Questionnaire

Career Drivers Questionnaire

What are your drivers? How do they influence your career? Complete the questionnaire below to help you assess your own career drivers.

There are no right and wrong answers. You have a total of 50 points. Allocate ten points—no more, no less, between the nine items in each of the five sections. If you wish, you may allocate ten points to one item if the other items in the section are of no importance to you.

SECTION ONE

These things are important to me:

1. ☐ I seek a high standard of living.
2. ☐ I wish to influence others.
3. ☐ I only feel satisfied if the output from my job has real value in itself.
4. ☐ I want to be an expert in the things I do.
5. ☐ I seek to be creative at work.
6. ☐ I strive to work only with people I like.
7. ☐ I choose jobs where I am "my own boss."
8. ☐ I take steps to be 100% financially secure.
9. ☐ I want to acquire a social status that other people will respect.

SECTION TWO

In my working life I want to:

10. ☐ become an expert in a chosen field.
11. ☐ build close relationships with others at work.
12. ☐ become a leader in teams and organizations.
13. ☐ be part of "the establishment."
14. ☐ make decisions that I really believe in.
15. ☐ get the highest paid jobs.
16. ☐ have a job with long-term security.
17. ☐ make my own decisions about how I spend my time at work.
18. ☐ create things that people associate with me alone.

Source: © Garrat, B. & Frances, D. (1994) *Managing Your Own Career*, HarperCollins Publisher Ltd.

SECTION THREE

If I am considering a new career opportunity:

19. ☐ I am drawn to roles with high social status.
20. ☐ I wish to be seen as a real specialist in my field.
21. ☐ I want to work to make a contribution to the wider community.
22. ☐ I want to look ahead at life and feel that I will always be okay.
23. ☐ I seek influence over others.
24. ☐ I wish to build warm personal relationships with people at work.
25. ☐ I want a high standard of living.
26. ☐ I want a degree of control over my own job.
27. ☐ producing things that bear my name attracts me.

SECTION FOUR

I would be disappointed if:

28. ☐ my work was not part of my "search for meaning" in life.
29. ☐ I did not practice highly skilled work.
30. ☐ I could not afford a high standard of living.
31. ☐ my job gave no opportunity to create something new or different.
32. ☐ I did not know where I would stand on retirement day.
33. ☐ I worked without friends.
34. ☐ I did not receive recognition or honors.
35. ☐ I had to refer to others for decisions.
36. ☐ I wasn't in charge of people.

SECTION FIVE

A "good" job means to me:

37. ☐ avoiding being a cog in a big wheel.
38. ☐ an excellent income.
39. ☐ plenty of time to study specialist subjects.
40. ☐ being a person who makes important decisions.
41. ☐ producing products or services that have my name on them.
42. ☐ having good relationships with other people.
43. ☐ being "in charge" of others.
44. ☐ being secure.
45. ☐ doing what I believe is important.

Appendix 7: Sample Proposal

Title:
A study of the correlation between students' understanding of the concepts of critical thinking, and their performance in synthesizing sources into an academic text.

Rationale for the study:
International students find great difficulty in effectively incorporating material from a range of sources. There are a number of key factors which influence this ability, one of which is obviously linguistic ability. Another less tangible factor is that of understanding the conventions of critical thinking, as understood in US academic studies.

This research will attempt to identify students' perceptions of critical thinking and their knowledge of the concept. It will then attempt to analyze if there is a correlation between this understanding and the ability to read, analyze and synthesize information.

Proposed research questions:
Is there a correlation between students' understanding of the process of critical thinking and their ability to select materials appropriately and incorporate these into their written work?

Do students of different cultural backgrounds have experience of different critical thinking skills?

Subjects/texts/sources of data

Questionnaires/interviews

Methods of data collection

Procedures

Methods of analysis

Problems which might be encountered

Appendix 8: Useful Language

Unit 1

Useful language: Reporting back

Our group thought the most controversial point was …

Point X provoked the most discussion.

Point X was the most controversial point.

There was some disagreement about point X.

Useful language: Agreeing and disagreeing

Absolutely. I totally agree.

Yes, that's true, but …

I'm not sure I agree with you there.

I agree up to a point, but …

Not necessarily.

That's a very good point.

Useful language: Signpost expressions (see also Appendix 1)

There are five main points which we consider important for successful study.

Our first point is …

Next, we have put …

Moving onto our third point, …

Fourthly, we think …

And finally, our last point is …

Useful language: Comparing perspectives

From (an instructor's) perspective, …

From the point of view of (the parents), …

If I were (the principal of the child's school), I'd probably feel that …

(The child psychologist) would argue that …

Useful language: Summarizing a discussion

Summing up your position

We finally all agreed that …

After much consideration, we decided that …

All things considered, we felt that …

On balance, we felt that …

We couldn't reach agreement on this issue.

Some of us felt that …, while others …

Recognizing strong arguments against your position

It's true that …

We recognized that …

We're fully aware that …

One has to acknowledge that …

Qualifying your position

This action should only be taken if …

So, although we agreed with the statement, we stressed that …

Useful language: Chairing a discussion

Getting started

Shall we begin?

Today, we're looking at the following question/topic …

Who would like to begin?

Clarification

So what you mean is …

If I've understood you correctly …

Managing contributions

Thanks, Pete, for your contribution …

OK, Pete, would anyone else like to comment?

Concluding

So, to sum up, …

We're running out of time, so …

Does anyone want to make a final point?

Have I forgotten anything?

Unit 3

Useful language: Referring to an article

This article deals with …

It provides …

The article reports that …

It refers to …

The article also gives statistics from …

According to the article …

The article then goes on to say that …

The article argues that …

It quotes …

The article reports on …

It doesn't mention …

Useful language: Exchanging opinions

Asking for opinions

What are your views on this issue?

Do you agree?

Presenting your own opinion

Well, I think …

It seems to me that …

In my view, …

Countering the other person's opinion

I take your point, but …

I understand what you're saying, but …

Well, I'm not sure if that's quite true …

But surely …

Useful language: Clarifying and confirming understanding

Confirming understanding as a listener

So what you're saying is …

So in your view, …

If I understand you correctly, you're saying …

Checking understanding as a speaker

Do you understand what I mean?

Do you follow what I am saying?

Am I making sense?

Showing that you do not understand

I'm not sure I understand what you mean.

I didn't quite follow you. Could you explain that point again, please?

Could you repeat that, please?

Unit 5

Useful language: Referring to data

This graph gives information about …

This line here shows …

This chart describes …

As these figures illustrate, …

This chart clearly shows that …

Useful language: Referring to other speakers

When you say … do you mean that …?

As you said, …

You made an interesting point about …

Following on from that point, …

Regarding what you both say about …

Can I also pick up on your point about …?

Those are fair arguments, but you make the point that …

As I said before, …

Unit 7

Useful language: Taking your turn

You want to make a point that is relevant at this moment in the discussion. You need to enter the discussion politely, but firmly:

Can I just jump in here?

You want to make a point, but the discussion moves on before you can contribute or finish. You can still make your point later:

To go back to my earlier point, …

Coming back to what John said earlier, …

I think I agree with the point you made earlier, Anne.

You start speaking at the same moment as another student. Both of you stop to let the other speak. It is polite to offer each other the chance to continue:

A: *Sorry, go on.*

B: *No, go ahead.*

A: *Thanks. I think …* [A makes his/her point and then invites B to speak] *Sorry, you were going to say …*

B: *Yes, I think …*

You notice that a quiet student is trying to speak, but other students keep speaking first. You can help the quiet student to get the attention of the group:

I think David has been trying to make a point.

David, did you want to make a point?

Useful language: Expressing quantity

Most Nearly all		of those interviewed/questioned …	reported/
Approximately Approaching Just under Just over	half a third 50 per cent	of the subjects … of the respondents …	stated/ claimed that …

Useful language: Expressing doubt and belief

I don't believe in this/these!

They don't exist.

It can't possibly be true …

It might be true …

There might be something in it.

I believe it does/might work.

Appendix 9: Photocopiable Handouts

Appendix 9a: Presentation assessment

Name of presenter	
Pronunciation of sounds/words	not clear reasonably clear clear very clear
Intonation	not varied quite varied varied
Volume	too quiet appropriate
Speed	too fast too slow appropriate
Eye contact	none too little reasonable good very good

Other comments

Appendix 9b: Discussion review

Participant

Name				
Did you ...	**1**	contribute to the discussion?	Yes	No
		If yes, how much? If no, why not?		
	2	listen and respond to what others said?	Yes	No
	3	encourage others to speak?	Yes	No
	4	refer to any of the points from the articles?	Yes	No
	5	feel the group reached a balanced conclusion, acknowledging different perspectives?	Yes	No
	6	use any of the useful language from this unit?	Yes	No

Chairperson

Name				
Did you ...	**1**	feel that you managed the discussion effectively?	Yes	No
	2	enjoy your role as chairperson?	Yes	No
	3	use any of the "useful language"?	Yes	No
	4	feel the group reached a balanced conclusion, acknowledging different perspectives?	Yes	No
What was difficult for you as chairperson?				

Appendix 9c: Presentation assessment

Name of presenter		
Was the topic clearly identified at the beginning?	Yes	No
Were the main points of the article clearly explained?	Yes	No
Did the presenter give his/her own views on the article?	Yes	No
Did the presenter explain the meaning of any difficult or technical words?	Yes	No
Was the visual aid helpful?	Yes	No
Suggestions for improvement		

Appendix 9d: Discussion review

Group members		
1	Did everyone in the group contribute to the discussion?	Yes No
2	Did group members encourage each other to speak?	Yes No
3	How could the group improve the next discussion?	
4	Did you make sure that people understood what you were saying?	Yes No
5	Did you indicate when you did not understand?	Yes No
6	Did you refer to any of the points from the articles in your discussion?	Yes No
7	Were you satisfied with your own participation in the discussion? (Why? Why not?)	
8	How could you improve your participation in the next discussion?	

Appendix 9e: Discussion review

1	Did everyone in the group contribute to the discussion?	Yes / No
2	Did group members encourage each other to speak?	Yes / No
3	Did speakers refer to points made by other group members?	Yes / No
4	Do you feel the discussion had a sense of direction?	Yes / No
5	How could the group improve the next discussion?	
6	Did you use any of the useful language for referring to other speakers?	Yes / No
7	Were you satisfied with your participation in the discussion?	Yes / No
	Why? Why not?	
8	How could you improve your participation in the next discussion?	
9	Did your ideas change during the discussion?	Yes / No
	If so, how did they change?	

Appendix 9f: Assessing class leader's role: Check list

1	Was the discussion topic appropriate, for example, a topic of interest to the group, and one they could participate in?	Yes / No
	Please comment	

2	Did the class leader give enough information about the topic in the beginning?	Yes / No
	Please comment	

3	Did the leader manage the class successfully? For example: —keep the discussion going; —allow everyone the opportunity to speak; —ensure one individual did not dominate.	Yes / No
	Please comment	

4	In what way could the class discussion have been improved?
	Please comment

Appendix 9g: Audience feedback sheet

How clearly did the speakers present their ideas?

Does it seem like a worthwhile proposal or experiment?

Can you see any problems in the experiment/proposal?

Overall comment

Pronunciation

Introduction

EAS: Pronunciation has been designed with the aims of helping you to:

- improve the accuracy of your pronunciation;
- develop your listening micro-skills;
- learn the phonemic alphabet;
- build your understanding of sound/spelling relationships;
- recognize and remember words and phrases that commonly occur in academic contexts.

Accuracy of pronunciation

Accurate pronunciation is important if you want people to understand you clearly. Frequent pronunciation errors may put a strain on the listener, and may also lead to breakdowns in communication. While you do not have to speak with a perfect English accent, your aim must be at least for your pronunciation to be good enough for the listener to understand you with ease. The main technique you can use to achieve this is to listen and repeat patterns of pronunciation, but learning the phonemic alphabet and developing a sensitive ear will also help you. If you are using this book with an instructor, his or her feedback will help you to identify which aspects of pronunciation you need to focus on, and what progress you are making in improving your pronunciation.

Learning the phonemic alphabet

The phonemic alphabet is a system for showing the pronunciation of words in English, and is shown on page 139 of this book. At first glance, the phonemic alphabet looks like another language that you have to learn. However, about half of the 44 phonemic symbols that you are expected to know are pronounced in the same way as they are written. In *EAS: Pronunciation* we have focused on:

- those <u>symbols</u> which may be unfamiliar, and so may be difficult to learn;
- those <u>sounds</u> which may be difficult to pronounce for certain students.

We believe that learning the phonemic alphabet will help you to develop more accurate pronunciation and improve your listening skills. In addition, if you know the phonemic alphabet you can:

- understand the correct pronunciation when looking up a word in a dictionary;
- note down the correct pronunciation in your vocabulary notebook.

So, knowing the phonemic alphabet is another important aspect of recording and learning vocabulary.

Listening micro-skills

In listening classes, you will have had practice understanding meaning that is built up over a sentence or several sentences, but you may have had difficulty with comprehension at a lower level. Listening micro-skills are the skills you need to understand meaning at the level of a word or small group of words.

Students frequently remark that there are many words that they know in their written form, but fail to recognize when listening. There may be several reasons for this; for example, words may not be pronounced in the way you expect them to be, or it may be difficult to hear where one word ends and another begins. Many activities in this book will help you to deal with such problems.

Sound/spelling relationships

Another difficulty faced by students is that there does not seem to be a relationship between the way words are spelled in English and the way they are pronounced. This creates problems, not just for accurate pronunciation, but also for correct spelling. In fact, while there are exceptions (and many of these exceptions seem to relate to the most common words in English), there are a lot of useful sound/spelling patterns. If you can ensure that you are familiar with these patterns, you can then focus on learning the exceptions, which are the words that create the most problems.

Academic vocabulary

The examples and exercises in these materials are focused on words from:

- the General Service List (GSL): the 2,000 most frequently used words in English;
- the Academic Word List (AWL): a list of 570 word families that are most commonly used in academic contexts.

All the words in the AWL will be useful to you, but some of the words in the GSL are either words you may know already (e.g., *you*, *from*, *hand*) or words that are not commonly or widely used in academic contexts (e.g., *handkerchief*, *niece*, *jealous*). In general, words like these have not been used in the examples and exercises.

In addition, a number of extracts from academic lectures have been used to provide practice in listening for features of pronunciation.

A lot of care has been taken, therefore, to ensure that the vocabulary focused on in this book is relevant to both academic study and your needs. Many words will be those you "half know," so the materials should reinforce your understanding. Other words may be quite new to you.

Using the materials

There is a range of different exercises that require you to work in different ways. For example, you may need to:

- listen and repeat words or sentences;
- stop the recording and read an explanation;
- stop the recording, write words in spaces in sentences, then listen to make sure your answers are correct;
- stop the recording, fill in a table or choose the correct answer, then listen to make sure your answers are correct.

If you just play the recording non-stop, listening and reading at the same time, you will not improve your pronunciation or listening skills. You will have to stop the recording to read, think, write and make sure your answers are correct, and you will have to replay short sections you have difficulty with.

Recording your own voice

When you are asked to listen and repeat words, phrases or sentences, it can also be very useful to record your own voice and then play it back. This will enable you to compare your own pronunciation with the recording, and hear any differences or problems clearly. You will not need to record your voice for every exercise, but try to do this when you know you have a problem with certain aspects of pronunciation.

If you are unsure whether your pronunciation on an exercise is accurate enough, and you are working with an instructor, ask him or her to listen to your recording. He or she will be able to assess your pronunciation more objectively.

Phonemic Alphabet

p

Consonants							
/p/	/t/	/k/	/s/	/ʃ/	/tʃ/	/f/	/θ/
post	take	keep	snow	shoe	choice	leaf	thin
/b/	/d/	/g/	/z/	/ʒ/	/dʒ/	/v/	/ð/
book	doctor	goal	zero	measure	jump	leave	the
/h/	/m/	/n/	/ŋ/	/l/	/r/	/w/	/j/
hotel	meet	nine	bring	late	red	well	yes

Vowels					
/æ/	/e/	/ɪ/	/ɒ/	/ʌ/	/ə/
plan	end	big	job	sum	the
/ʊ/	/ɑ:/	/ɜ:/	/i:/	/ɔ:/	/u:/
good	car	her	fee	law	too

Diphthongs							
/aɪ/	/aʊ/	/oʊ/	/eɪ/	/eə/	/ɪə/	/ɔɪ/	/ʊə/
why	now	go	day	care	dear	enjoy	pure

Notes:

1. The sound /ə/ is very common in unstressed syllables in English.
   In this sentence it occurs seven times: *Poverty is at the center of the problem.*

2. The sound /ʊə/ is relatively uncommon in English.

3. Many vowel or diphthong sounds can be spelled in different ways, e.g., /ɜ:/ in *her, turn, heard, word*, and many similar spellings can be pronounced in different ways, e.g., *head* /hed/, *heat* /hi:t/, *heart* /hɑ:rt/, *heard* /hɜ:rd/.

1 Vowel Sounds 1, Word Stress and Weak Forms

In this unit you will:
- learn which phonemic symbols represent certain vowel sounds;
- practice recognizing and producing these vowel sounds;
- learn about the concepts of the syllable and word stress;
- practice producing words with the correct word stress;
- practice recognizing weak forms of function words when listening.

These are the 12 vowel sounds in English. In this unit, we will focus on the six sounds shaded in this table.

/æ/	/e/	/ɪ/	/ɒ/	/ʌ/	/ə/
pl<u>a</u>n	<u>e</u>nd	b<u>i</u>g	j<u>o</u>b	s<u>u</u>m	th<u>e</u>

/ʊ/	/ɑː/	/ɜː/	/iː/	/ɔː/	/uː/
g<u>oo</u>d	c<u>ar</u>	h<u>er</u>	f<u>ee</u>	l<u>aw</u>	t<u>oo</u>

Task 1: Vowel sounds

1.1 🎧 CD1 – 1 **Listen to the difference in the pronunciation of these pairs of words. In each of them, the vowel sound is different.**

a) /ɪ/   /iː/
   fit   feet
   dip   deep
   hit   heat

c) /æ/   /ɑː/
   hat   heart
   match   march
   pack   park

b) /æ/   /e/
   mass   mess
   band   bend
   had   head

d) /e/   /ɜː/
   ten   turn
   head   heard
   went   weren't

Listen again and repeat the words.

1.2 🎧 CD1 – 2 **You will hear some of the words from Ex 1.1. Listen and circle the phonemic transcription that matches the pronunciation of the word you hear.**

Example: /hed/ (/hɜːrd/)

a) /pæk/   /pɑːrk/
b) /ten/   /tɜːrn/
c) /mæs/   /mes/
d) /hɪt/   /hiːt/
e) /went/   /wɜːrnt/

f) /dɪp/   /diːp/
g) /hæd/   /hed/
h) /hæt/   /hɑːrt/
i) /bænd/   /bend/

1.3   CD1 – 3 **Listen to six more words and do the following exercises.**

a) Listen and circle the phonemic transcription that matches the pronunciation of the word you hear.

1 /sɪt/ _____   /siːt/ _____

2 /mæt/ _____   /met/ _____

3 /hɜːrt/ _____   /hɑːrt/ _____

4 /fɑːr/ _____   /fɜːr/ _____

5 /lɪv/ _____   /liːv/ _____

6 /sæd/ _____   /sed/ _____

b) Write the words, with the correct spelling, in the spaces next to the phonemic transcriptions.

Task 2: Syllables

For pronunciation purposes, words can be divided into syllables. A syllable contains only one vowel sound, which may be preceded or followed by consonants. Remember that some consonants are pronounced as vowels; for example, *heavy* is a two-syllable word, because the *y* is pronounced as a vowel.

2.1   CD1 – 4 **Listen to these examples of words with one, two and three or more syllables.**

a) one-syllable words

> aid   quote   source   fee

b) two-syllable words

> cred•it   ac•cept   heav•y   e•quate

c) words with three or more syllables

> pol•i•cy (3)   sim•i•lar (3)   en•vi•ron•ment (4)   i•den•ti•fy (4)   in•di•vid•ual (4)

2.2   CD1 – 5 **Listen to these words and decide how many syllables there are in each of them.**

	Syllables			Syllables
a) specific	_____	**f)** consequent	_____
b) alter	_____	**g)** framework	_____
c) resource	_____	**h)** significant	_____
d) preliminary	_____	**i)** adapt	_____
e) available	_____	**j)** differentiate	_____

Pronunciation note

There is some variation in the way people pronounce words. For example, some people pronounce *preliminary* with four syllables – /prɪˈlɪmɪnrɪ/, while other people pronounce it with five syllables – /prɪˈlɪmɪnərɪ/.

Task 3: Word stress patterns

In words of more than one syllable, one syllable is emphasized more than others; it has a stronger sound than other syllables.

3.1 ⊙ **CD1 – 6 Listen for the stressed syllable in these words.**
The stressed syllable is marked with (').

> 'pol•i•cy   'sim•i•lar   en•'vi•ron•ment   i•'den•ti•fy   in•di•'vid•ual
> as•'sume   'ma•jor   o•ver•'seas   op•e•'ra•tion   re•in•'force

3.2 ⊙ **CD1 – 7 Listen again to the words from Ex 2.2. Mark the stressed syllables as shown in the following example.**

Example: a) spe'cific

3.3 ⊙ **CD1 – 8 Listen to the following sentences and mark the stressed syllable in the words in bold.**

a) The **protection** of children is the main **purpose** of this legislation.

b) The samples were **analyzed** in the lab.

c) Chemical **analysis** of the rock provided surprising results.

d) The aim of the study was to **identify** the **factors** contributing to domestic violence.

e) **Periodicals** are kept in an area on the ground floor.

f) The **administration** of these drugs needs to be closely monitored.

g) In **percentage** terms, this is not a significant increase.

h) This is the standard **procedure** for limiting spread of the disease.

Task 4: Strong and weak forms of function words

4.1 ⊙ **CD1 – 9 Listen to these pairs of sentences. What is the difference in the pronunciation of the words in bold in each pair? How can you explain this difference?**

a) 1 Interest rates **are** rising.
2 No, that's not true. We **are** doing something about it.

b) 1 Would you like **some** tea?
2 Most scientists are convinced about global warming, but **some** are not.

c) 1 Where's he coming **from**?
2 Results differed **from** one region to another.

d) 1 Is that **your** pen or mine?
2 Can I borrow **your** dictionary?

Pronunciation note

Ex 4.1 shows that the pronunciation of some one-syllable function words may be different when these words are *unstressed* (or *weak*) in a sentence, compared with their pronunciation when they are *stressed* (or *strong*). Function words are very common words (including conjunctions, pronouns, prepositions, articles, determiners and auxiliary and modal verbs) that do not seem to have much meaning, but are used to show relationships between vocabulary words or to modify their meaning. Very often, the vowel sound in unstressed function words is /ə/.

In the sentences in Ex 4.1, you will see that function words are *stressed* when they *add emphasis*, e.g., *No, that's not true. We **are** doing something about it.* This is also done to *indicate a contrast*, e.g., *Most scientists are convinced..., but **some** are not.* You may also notice that function words at the end of sentences or questions have a strong form.

Here are some examples of these function words and their different pronunciations.

	Stressed/Strong	Unstressed/Weak
but	/bʌt/	/bət/
than	/ðæn/	/ðən/
them	/ðem/	/ðəm/
you	/juː/	/jə/
at	/æt/	/ət/
for	/fɔːr/	/fər/
the	/ðiː/	/ðə/
some	/sʌm/	/səm/
has	/hæz/	/həz/, /əz/
does	/dʌz/	/dəz/
can	/kæn/	/kən/

4.2 🎧 **CD1 – 10 Listen to these sentences and write in the missing words, which are all weak forms of function words.**

a) One criticism leveled _____ the board was their lack _____ financial control.

b) This issue was discussed _____ some length during the conference.

c) These points should _____ been made more effectively.

d) How do we account _____ this change in behavior?

e) This might do more harm _____ good.

f) This kind of restructuring is usually regarded by employees _____ a change _____ the worse.

g) This problem _____ easily be solved _____ minimal cost.

h) Trade sanctions will be imposed with effect from the 1ˢᵗ _____ December.

4.3 ⊙ CD1 – 11 **Study the following introduction to a lecture on globalization. Then listen and write in the missing words, which again are weak forms of function words.**

Well, as Ros said, I'm going to talk about globalization today, which is one _____ the catch phrases or buzzwords, if you like, _____ the late 20ᵗʰ _____ early 21ˢᵗ centuries. It's constantly in _____ news. It's used by politicians, by people in _____ media, by business people, and when they're referring _____ globalization they talk about things like _____ way we _____ communicate almost instantaneously nowadays with people on the other side _____ _____ world by e-mail or by telephone. They're also talking about, _____ example, the way that _____ fall in share prices in one part _____ _____ world, _____ example in the Far East, _____ have an immediate impact on the stock markets on the other side _____ _____ world, like in London _____ Frankfurt.

4.4 ⊙ CD1 – 12 **Listen to these phrases and repeat them. Can you identify and produce the weak forms of the function words?**

a) past and present figures

b) more or less fifty

c) they were selected at random

d) it was far from clear

e) the results of the trials

f) too good to be true

g) needless to say

h) it's gone from bad to worse

i) we'll have to wait and see

j) we had some problems

Unit Summary

In this unit, you have learned six English vowel sounds: /ɪ/, /iː/, /e/, /ɜː/, /æ/, /ɑː/, and practiced their pronunciation. You have also become more aware of syllables and word stress, and practiced listening for weak forms of function words.

1   **Say the words in the box aloud. Decide how many syllables there are in each word and write them in the correct spaces below.**

globalization   century   constantly   politician   refer   media   financial   market

a)   two-syllable words: _____   _____

b)   three-syllable words: _____   _____   _____   _____

c)   four-syllable words: _____

d)   five-syllable words: _____

2   🎧 CD1 – 13 **Now listen to the words from Ex 1 and mark the stressed syllable in each word.**

3   **Which of the stressed syllables from Ex 2 have the following vowel sounds?**

Note: Only six of the words contain these sounds.

/ɪ/,   /iː/,   /e/,   /ɜː/,   /æ/,   /ɑː/

4   **Which words in these sentences would usually be pronounced using a weak form?**

a)   Globalization is one of the buzzwords of the twenty-first century.

b)   It's constantly in the news and is often referred to by politicians and the media.

c)   A fall in share prices in one part of the world can have an impact on the stock markets on the other side of the world.

5   **Think about the questions below.**

a)   Why do you think students confuse some of the vowel sounds you have practiced in this unit?

b)   Why is it useful to note the stressed syllable when you learn a new multi-syllable word?

c)   How can you check the correct stress and number of syllables of words you learn?

For web resources, see:
www.englishforacademicstudy.com/us/student/pronunciation/links

These weblinks will provide you with further practice in areas of pronunciation such as the sounds, stress, and intonation patterns of English.

Vowel Sounds 2, Word Stress Patterns

In this unit you will:
- learn which phonemic symbols represent the other vowel sounds;
- practice recognizing and producing these vowel sounds;
- learn more about which syllable is stressed in some types of word.

In Unit 1, we looked at six vowel sounds. In this unit, we will focus on the other six vowel sounds shaded in this table.

/æ/	/e/	/ɪ/	/ɒ/	/ʌ/	/ə/
pl<u>a</u>n	<u>e</u>nd	b<u>ig</u>	j<u>ob</u>	s<u>u</u>m	th<u>e</u>

/ʊ/	/ɑː/	/ɜː/	/iː/	/ɔː/	/uː/
<u>goo</u>d	<u>car</u>	h<u>er</u>	f<u>ee</u>	l<u>aw</u>	t<u>oo</u>

Task 1: Vowel sounds

1.1 🎧 **CD1 – 14 Listen to the difference in the pronunciation of these pairs of words. In each of them, the vowel sound is different.**

a) /æ/

match
lack
ankle

The mouth is relaxed and quite wide open. The sound comes from the front of the mouth.

/ʌ/

much
luck
uncle

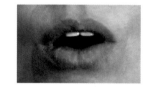

The mouth is open and slightly rounded. The sound comes from the middle of the mouth.

b) /ʊ/

pull
soot
full

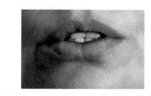

The lips are slightly rounded and pushed forwards. The sound comes from between the middle and the back of the mouth.

/uː/

pool
suit
fool

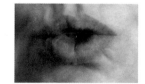

The lips are rounded and pushed forwards. The sound comes from the back of the mouth.

c) /ɒ/

spot
shot
stock

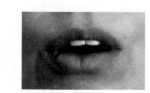

The mouth is slightly rounded and quite open. The sound comes from the back of the mouth.

/ɔː/

sport
short
stork

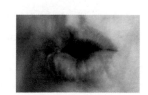

The mouth is rounded and the lips are pushed forward. The tongue is near the roof of the mouth and the sound comes from the back of the mouth.

d) /ɒ/

lock
box
shock

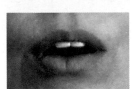

/ʊ/

look
books
shook

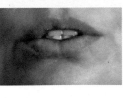

Listen again and repeat the words.

1.2 ⊙ CD1 – 15 **You will hear some of the words from Ex 1.1. Listen and circle the phonemic transcription that matches the pronunciation of the word you hear.**

Example: (/læk/) /lʌk/

a)	/bɒks/	/bʊks/	**f)**	/fʊl/	/fuːl/
b)	/pʊl/	/puːl/	**g)**	/lɒk/	/lʌk/
c)	/spɒt/	/spɪt/	**h)**	/stɒk/	/stɔːk/
d)	/mætʃ/	/mʌtʃ/	**i)**	/ʃɒt/	/ʃɔːrt/
e)	/ænkəl/	/ʌnkəl/			

1.3 ⊙ CD1 – 16 **Listen to six more words and do the following exercises.**

a) Listen and circle the phonemic transcription that matches the pronunciation of the word you hear.

1 /fæn/ _____ /fʌn/ _____

2 /muːd/ _____ /mʌd/ _____

3 /kuːl/ _____ /kɔːl/ _____

4 /buːt/ _____ /bɔːt/ _____

5 /fʊt/ _____ /fuːd/ _____

6 /kʊd/ _____ /kɑːrd/ _____

b) Write the words, with the correct spelling, in the spaces next to the phonemic transcriptions.

Task 2: Unstressed syllables: /ə/ and /ɪ/

Short /ə/

The mouth is relaxed and slightly open. The sound comes from the middle of the mouth.

The short /ə/ sound *only* appears in *unstressed* syllables. As can be seen from the examples given on the next page, there is no single written vowel form to represent /ə/. At the end of words, it may appear in written form as ~*er*, ~*re*, ~*our*, or ~*or* (as in *reader, meager, favor* and *actor*). (Note: Many words ending with ~*or* in American English end with ~*our* in British English: fav*or*/fav*our*, flav*or*/flav*our*, harb*or*/harb*our*, etc.)

2.1 🎧 CD1 – 17 **Listen to these examples.**

> appear /əˈpɪər/   suggest /səˈdʒest/   effort /ˈefərt/   color /ˈkʌlər/

2.2 **Study the words 1–14 and do the following activities.**

a) Mark the stressed syllable with (').

b) Write /ə/ above any syllables that include this sound.

c) 🎧 CD1 – 18 Listen and repeat the words.

Example: cŏmˈputĕr

1 affect

2 several

3 standard

4 failure

5 purpose

6 propose

7 author

8 attempt

9 distance

10 accept

11 opposite

12 flavour

13 compare

14 approach

Short /ɪ/

The tongue is quite close to the roof of the mouth and the lips are stretched. The sound comes from the front of the mouth.

In unstressed syllables where the vowel letter is written as e, it is often pronounced as a short /ɪ/.

2.3 🎧 CD1 – 19 **Listen to these examples.**

> describe /dɪsˈkraɪb/
>
> prefer /prɪˈfɜːr/

2.4 **Study the words 1–7 and do the following activities.**

a) Mark the stressed syllable with (').

b) Write /ɪ/ above any syllables that include this sound.

c) 🎧 CD1 – 20 Listen and repeat the words.

Example: rĕˈduce

1   invited

2   decision

3   demand

4   beyond

5   extensive

6   research

7   interpret

Task 3: Word stress patterns

Groups of nouns, adjectives and verbs with similar endings (or suffixes) often follow similar word stress patterns. In the groups of words below, the stress falls on the syllable *before* the ending (e.g., ~sion, ~tion, ~graphy).

3.1   ⊕ **CD1 – 21 Listen and repeat the following words, making sure you stress the syllables in the columns highlighted in the tables below.**

Nouns ending in ~*sion* or ~*tion*

discussion

solution

occasion

definition

decision

position

dis	CUS	sion
so	LU	tion
oc	CA	sion
defi	NI	tion
de	CI	sion
po	SI	tion

Nouns ending in ~*graphy*

geography

biography

photography

ge	O	graphy
bi	O	graphy
pho	TO	graphy

Adjectives ending in ~*ic*

electric

economic

specific

e	LEC	tric
eco	NO	mic
spe	CI	fic

Nouns ending in ~*ency* or ~*ancy*

frequency

consultancy

consistency

vacancy

efficiency

redundancy

	FRE	quency
con	SUL	tancy
con	SIS	tency
	VA	cancy
ef	FI	ciency
re	DUN	dancy

Nouns ending in ~*ium*

medium

uranium

consortium

	ME	dium
u	RA	nium
con	SOR	tium

Adjectives ending in ~ical

electrical
political
periodical

e	LEC	trical
po	LI	tical
peri	O	dical

Nouns ending in ~ity

identity
authority
community

i	DEN	tity
au	THO	rity
com	MU	nity

Adjectives ending in ~tial or ~cial

essential
financial
potential
commercial
residential
artificial

es	SEN	tial
fi	NAN	cial
po	TEN	tial
com	MER	cial
resi	DEN	tial
arti	FI	cial

Verbs ending in ~ify

modify
clarify
identify

	MO	dify
	CLA	rify
i	DEN	tify

Nouns ending in ~logy

apology
technology
biology

a	PO	logy
tech	NO	logy
bi	O	logy

Adjectives ending in ~tional

additional
international
optional

a	DDI	tional
inter	NA	tional
	OP	tional

3.2 **Study the words 1–12 and do the following activities.**

a) Mark the stressed syllable in each word, following the patterns in Ex 3.1.

b) 🎧 **CD1 – 22** Listen to make sure your answers are correct. Repeat the words to practice your pronunciation.

1 academic

2 dimension

3 beneficial

4 similarity

5 majority

6 initial

7 demography

8 allergic

9 tradition

10 deficiency

11 conventional

12 justify

3.3 **Study the sentences below. Use words from Ex 3.1 to complete the sentences.**

a) Most of the course units are mandatory, but there are two _____ units.

b) The committee hasn't made a _____ whether or not to award funding for the project.

c) It's important to start with a _____ of the term "sustainable development," as it clearly means different things to different people.

d) Although solar power provides a _____ answer to some of the world's energy needs, at the moment the technology is quite expensive.

e) Have we really found a _____ to the problem?

f) It's hoped that the development of _____ intelligence will mean that computers will be able to think in the way humans do.

g) There's a lot of confusion, so it's essential to _____ the situation.

h) The stadium was built by an international _____ of construction companies.

i) There's a _____ for a laboratory technician, so the post will be advertised next week.

j) James Watson's _____ of Margaret Thatcher was published last month.

k) The organization plans to publish a new _____, with three issues a year.

l) Despite plans for _____ growth of five percent over the next year, unemployment is continuing to rise.

m) We'll need to _____ the design of the equipment after a number of weaknesses were discovered in the testing process.

n) Professor Jones is a leading _____ on 17th-century Italian literature.

o) The _____ areas of the new town will be located well away from the industrial and commercial zones.

🎧 **CD1 – 23 Now listen to make sure your answers are correct.**

Practice your pronunciation by playing the recording again and pausing to repeat the sentences.

Task 4: Word families: Word stress and pronunciation

Word families are groups of words that have the same basic form and similar meanings. By adding prefixes or suffixes, you can generate nouns, adjectives, adverbs and verbs from the basic form. Learning word families is a useful technique for extending your range of vocabulary.

Word stress

In many cases, the word stress pattern does not change from one form of the word to another.

4.1 CD1 – 24 **Listen to the following examples.**

Verb	Noun	Adjective
poss'ess	poss'ession	poss'essive
per'suade	per'suasion	per'suasive
ass'ess	ass'essment	ass'essed

However, in some cases the word stress may vary from one form to another. For example:

'analyze (v),   an'alysis (n),   ana'lytical (adj)

4.2 CD1 – 25 **Listen and repeat these words. Mark the stressed syllable. The first one is done for you.**

Verb	Noun	Adjective
ap'ply	appli'cation	ap'plicable
activate	activity	active
inform	information	informative
–	probability	probable
socialize	society	social
experiment	experiment	experimental
equal	equality	equal
unite	union	united
transfer	transfer	transferable

You may also notice differences in the vowel or consonant sounds. For example, in *social* /ˈsəʊʃl/ and *society* /səˈsaɪəti/, the first vowel sound is different in each word.

Even when the word stress does not change, there may be differences in pronunciation of the basic form.

4.3 CD1 – 26 **Listen to these examples.**

occur (*v*)   /əˈkɜːr/   occurrence (*n*) /əˈkʌrəns/
assume (*v*) /əˈsuːm/   assumption (*n*) /əˈsʌmpʃən/

4.4 **Study the groups of sentences below and do activities a) and b).**

a) Complete the blanks with a form of the word printed in bold in the first sentence.

b) Mark the stressed syllable in the words that you write in the blanks.

Example:

We need to **'analyze** the data.
Statistical <u>an'alysis</u> of the data provided some unexpected results.
You need good <u>ana'lytical</u> skills for this kind of work.

1 The stomach **pro'duces** acids, which help to digest food.
   The new model should be in _____ in November.
   If the factory doesn't become more _____, it faces closure.
   The _____ was withdrawn from sale after a number of defects were identified.

2 Four alternate **'methods** of payment are offered.
   She takes a very _____ approach to her work.
   They've been developing a new _____ for research in this area.

3 The president stated that **eco'nomic** development was the main priority.
   The dean is concerned that the _____ is overheating.
   She is studying _____ at Georgetown University.

4 Wages tend to be higher in the **'private** sector.
   This law is intended to protect people's _____ .
   The water services industry was _____ in the 1980s.

5 The heights of plants **'varied** from 8 cm to 15 cm.
   A wide _____ of fruit is grown on the island.
   Regional _____ in the unemployment rate are significant.
   A number of _____, such as wind speed and direction, humidity and air pressure,
   need to be considered.

6 Both approaches yielded **'similar** results.
   There are many _____ between the two religions.
   The firefighters resorted to industrial action to settle the dispute. _____, railway
   workers are threatening to strike because of changes in working practices.

4.5 ⊙ CD1 – 27 **Listen to the sentences and correct any that you got wrong.**

In this unit, you have learned six English vowel sounds: /ɒ/, /ʌ/, /ə/, /ʊ/, /ɔː/, /uː/, and practiced their pronunciation. You have also become more aware of weak forms and looked at different word stress patterns.

1 🎧 **CD1 – 28 Listen to the words in the box. Then match them to the phonemic transcriptions below.**

> other   ankle   pull   shot   uncle   pool   short   another

a) /ənʌðər/

b) /puːl/

c) /ʃɔːrt/

d) /pʊl/

e) /ʌŋkəl/

f) /æŋkəl/

g) /ʌðər/

h) /ʃɒt/

2 **Choose seven multi-syllable nouns that are connected with your field of study. (If you like, you can include words that you have already studied in this unit.) For each word, do the following:**

a) Write the word and mark the syllable that is stressed.

b) Check the pronunciation of the word in a dictionary. Do you pronounce the unstressed syllable(s) using the sounds /ə/ or /ɪ/?

c) Does the word belong to a word family? Write as many other related words as you can think of, e.g., verb and adjective forms or other nouns with the same root.

> For web resources, see:
>
> **www.englishforacademicstudy.com/us/student/pronunciation/links**
>
> These weblinks will provide you with further practice in areas of pronunciation such as the sounds, stress, and intonation patterns of English.

3

Consonant Sounds 1, Sentence Stress

In this unit you will:
- learn about the pronunciation of voiced and unvoiced consonants;
- practice recognizing and producing these sounds;
- learn to identify stressed words in sentences;
- practice using sentence stress to highlight important information.

Task 1: Voiced and unvoiced consonants

There are a number of pairs of consonants that are pronounced in the same way, except that one consonant is *unvoiced* and the other is *voiced*.

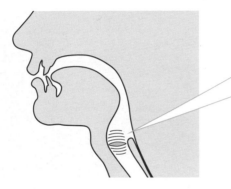

For **voiced** consonants /b/, /d/, /g/, etc., the vocal chords in your throat vibrate.

For **unvoiced** consonants /p/, /t/, /k/, etc., there is *no* vibration.

1.1 🎧 **CD1 – 29 Listen and repeat these continuous sounds.**

SSSSSSSSSSSSSSSSS

ZZZZZZZZZZZZZZZZZ

The position of your tongue, lips and mouth is more or less the same for each sound, but for the /z/ sound there is also vibration of your vocal chords, so we say that /z/ is a *voiced* consonant. There is no vibration for the /s/ sound, so it is *unvoiced*.

/s/ is **unvoiced**, e.g., s̲now

/z/ is **voiced**, e.g., z̲ero

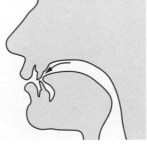

For both these sounds, the tip of the tongue is held close to the part of the mouth just above the teeth. There is a narrow gap through which you force air.

In the table on page 156, each pair of consonants (/p/ and /b/, /t/ and /d/, etc.) is pronounced in the same way, except that one is voiced and the other is unvoiced.

1.2 ⊙ CD1 – 30 **Listen and repeat each pair of words. Can you hear the difference in pronunciation?**

Unvoiced		Voiced	
/p/	p̲ie	/b/	b̲uy
/t/	t̲own	/d/	d̲own
/k/	c̲oal	/g/	g̲oal
/s/	s̲ink	/z/	z̲inc
/ʃ/	mes̲h̲	/ʒ/	meas̲ure
/tʃ/	c̲h̲unk	/dʒ/	j̲unk
/f/	f̲ast	/v/	v̲ast
/θ/	breat̲h̲	/ð/	breat̲h̲e

/ʃ/ is **unvoiced**, e.g., mes̲h̲

/ʒ/ is **voiced**, e.g., meas̲ure

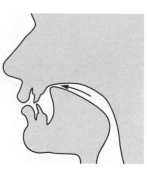

For both these sounds, the tongue is held close to the roof of the mouth. There is a narrow gap through which you force air. Compare these sounds with /s/ and /z/ on page 155. You will see the tongue is higher and further back in the mouth.

/f/ is **unvoiced**, e.g., f̲ast

/v/ is **voiced**, e.g., v̲ast

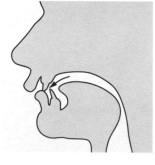

For both these sounds, the inside part of the bottom lip is held against the top teeth. Pressure is released as you bring the bottom lip away from the top teeth.

1.3 ⊙ CD1 – 31 **Look at the following pairs of words and circle the word you hear.**

Each pair is pronounced in the same way, except that one consonant is unvoiced and the other is voiced.

Example: pill   (bill)

	Unvoiced	Voiced
a)	paste	based
b)	simple	symbol
c)	tense	dense
d)	try	dry
e)	white	wide
f)	card	guard
g)	class	glass
h)	ankle	angle
i)	sown	zone
j)	price	prize
k)	use (*n*)	use (*v*)
l)	advice (*n*)	advise (*v*)
m)	rich	ridge
n)	batch	badge
o)	few	view
p)	proof (*n*)	prove (*v*)
q)	belief (*n*)	believe (*v*)

Make sure your answers are correct. Then listen and repeat the words with the correct voiced or unvoiced consonant.

1.4 🎧 **CD1 – 32 Listen and complete these sentences or phrases.**

a) **1** a _____ situation   ___

2 a _____ material   ___

b) **1** a _____ area   ___

2 as _____ as a sheet   ___

c) **1** at the _____ of the plant   ___

2 the _____ of change   ___

d) **1** Public _____ have improved.   ___

2 A cube has six _____.   ___

e) **1** difficult to _____   ___

2 It's had good _____.   ___

f) **1** the _____ of the fire   ___

2 It changed the _____ of his life.   ___

1.5 **Write *U* or *V* beside each sentence or phrase to show if the missing word has an unvoiced or a voiced consonant.**

Example: a <u>tense</u> situation <u>U</u>

1.6 **Listen again and repeat the sentences or phrases, focusing on accurate pronunciation.**

Task 2: /θ/, /t/ and /s/

2.1 ⊙ CD1 – 33 **Listen to the difference in pronunciation between these pairs of words.**

/θ/	/s/
thing	sing
path	pass
worth	worse
mouth	mouse
youth	use

/θ/	/t/
thin	tin
thank	tank
thread	tread
both	boat
death	debt

Listen again and repeat the words.

Pronunciation note

/θ/ is always written as *th* (*think*, *both*).

2.2 ⊙ CD1 – 34 **You will hear some of the words from Ex 2.1. Circle the phonemic transcription that matches the pronunciation of the word you hear.**

Example: /θɪn/   /tɪn/

a)	/θæŋk/	/tæŋk/
b)	/deθ/	/det/
c)	/bəʊθ/	/bəʊt/
d)	/wɜːrθ/	/wɜːrs/
e)	/pɑːθ/	/pɑːs/
f)	/maʊθ/	/maʊs/
g)	/juːθ/	/juːs/

2.3 **Complete these sentences with words from Ex 2.1.**

a) The painting is supposed to be _____ $5 million.

b) The fuel is stored in a 30-liter _____.

c) Cancer is the leading cause of _____ among women.

d) A _____ layer of plastic is needed to provide waterproofing.

e) I couldn't follow the _____ of his argument.

f) The _____ is, no one likes to be criticized.

g) Tax increases are necessary to finance the national _____.

2.4 ⊙ CD1 – 35 **Now listen to the correct answers and repeat the sentences.**

Task 3: /ð/

/ð/ occurs as the first sound in a number of common function words.

3.1 🎧 CD1 – 36 **Listen and repeat these words.**

the	this	these	that	those	they	their*
there*	theirs	than	then	though		

* These words have the same pronunciation.

Pronunciation note

/ð/ is always written as *th* (*this, other*).

This sound also occurs at the end of some common words as /ðər/, spelled ~*ther*.

weather**	whether**	gather	either	neither	together	bother	rather
other	another	further	mother	father	brother		

** These words have the same pronunciation.

3.2 🎧 CD1 – 37 **Listen to these sentences and phrases and repeat them.**

a) What's the weather like there?

b) Let's get together.

c) I'd rather not.

d) I wouldn't bother.

e) I don't like them.

f) I don't like them, either.

g) …: further down the road …

h) … the other day …

Task 4: /θ/ and /ð/

/θ/ is **unvoiced**, e.g., <u>th</u>in

/ð/ is **voiced**, e.g., <u>th</u>e

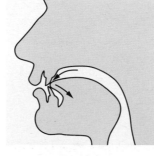

For both these sounds, the tip of the tongue is held against the back of the teeth. Pressure is released as you bring the tip of the tongue away from the teeth.

4.1 🎧 **CD1 – 38 Listen to these two words.**

thank	/θæŋk/
than	/ðæn/

To pronounce both /θ/ and /ð/, you put the tip of your tongue against the back of your teeth, but /ð/ is also *voiced*. Can you hear how /ð/ has a heavier sound than /θ/?

4.2 🎧 **CD1 – 39 Listen to these phrases and write in the correct symbols above the words.**

          ð θ

Example: … another thing to consider is …

a) … in theory …

b) … the truth is that …

c) … the growth rate …

d) … a further theme …

e) … they thought that ….

f) … this method …

g) … beneath the surface …

h) … this therapy might be used to …

i) … youth culture …

Now listen again and repeat the phrases.

Pronunciation note

If you find the /θ/ sound difficult to pronounce, people should still understand from the context if you replace it with the /s/ sound or the /t/ sound.

So, if you can't say …	try saying …
thank	*sank, tank*
thin	*sin, tin*
worth	*worse*

Similarly, if you find the /ð/ sound difficult to pronounce, people should still understand from the context if you replace it with the /z/ sound or the /d/ sound.

So, if you can't say …	try saying …
they	*day*
then	*zen, den*
breathe	*breeze*

Task 5: Sentence stress

While word stress (or accent) is generally decided by language rules, sentence stress (or prominence) is decided by speaker choice. The speaker usually chooses to stress content words, which carry the information, and not structure or function words, such as auxiliary verbs, pronouns, prepositions and determiners, although this is not always the case.

5.1   CD1 – 40 **Listen to this recording of the previous paragraph.**

You will hear that the underlined words sound stronger than the other words. These are the words that the speaker has chosen to stress.

While <u>word</u> stress (or <u>accent</u>) is generally decided by language <u>rules</u>, <u>sentence</u> stress (or <u>prominence</u>) is decided by <u>speaker</u> <u>choice</u>. The <u>speaker</u> usually chooses to stress <u>content</u> words, which carry the <u>information</u>, and not <u>structure</u> or <u>function</u> words, such as <u>auxiliary</u> verbs, <u>pronouns</u>, <u>prepositions</u>, and <u>determiners</u>, although this is not <u>always</u> the case.

5.2   CD1 – 41 **Listen to these sentences, in which the sentence stress changes according to the meaning.**

You **have** to hand in the essay on Monday   … there's a **strict deadline**.

You have to hand in the **essay** on Monday   … not the **report**.

You have to hand in the essay on **Monday**   … not **Wednesday**.

Practice repeating them with the correct sentence stress.

5.3   CD1 – 42 **Listen to these beginnings of sentences and choose the more suitable ending, according to the sentence stress.**

a) Well, we know how this happened, …

☐ … but do other people know?

☐ … but do we know why it happened?

b) Having looked at the effect of deforestation on the environment, …

☐ … we will now discuss greenhouse gases and the roles they play.

☐ … we will now consider its effect on the economy.

c) Most of our cotton is imported, …

☐ … but we produce about 500,000 tonnes a year.

☐ … but we are self-sufficient in wool.

d) The crime rate fell by 15 percent last year, …

☐ … but this year it's risen.

☐ … but this year the figure is nearer to 8 percent.

e) The oil pump needs replacing, …

☐ … not the filter.

☐ … as it can't be repaired.

5.4 🔊 **CD1 – 43 Now listen to the complete sentences to check your answers.**

Can you hear how words are contrasted through stress in different parts of each sentence?

5.5 🔊 **CD1 – 44 Read and listen to an extract from a lecture called *Introduction to British Agriculture*. Underline the words you hear stressed.**

> As a backdrop to all these activities, particularly after the Second World War, a lot of effort was put into research and development of agriculture in terms of plant breeding, breeding crops that were higher yielding, that were perhaps disease-resistant, and so on and so forth. Also, crops that might have better quality, better bread-making quality, higher gluten content, to make them doughy, higher protein content, and so on and so forth. Research, too, and this is again at one of the university farms, research into livestock production. Understanding how to better manage our livestock, again to make them produce more, certainly, but also to produce and influence the quality of the livestock products, whether that happens to be milk or cheese, come back to that in a moment, or indeed meat.

5.6 **Why do you think the speaker chose to stress those words? Listen to the extract again and repeat it sentence by sentence.**

5.7 🔊 **CD1 – 45 Read and listen to part of a lecture on globalization. Underline the words you hear stressed.**

> Now to get to the meat of the lecture, the basic purpose of this lecture is to give you some overview of the kind of contemporary academic and policy debate about globalization and particularly about a very specific, although rather general, debate itself, that's the debate on the effect of globalization on the role of the state. So, you see on the overhead, the lecture's going to be kind of in two parts: the first will be looking at globalization, causes and consequences, and more particularly a kind of definition of the discussion of some of the competing concepts of globalization, that is, you know, what people say it is, so that we can then discuss in some detail, hopefully, this question of how globalization is affecting the state.

5.8 **Why do you think the speaker chose to stress those words? Listen to the extract again and repeat it sentence by sentence.**

Unit Summary

In this unit, you have learned about voiced and unvoiced consonant sounds, practiced distinguishing between commonly confused sounds and focused on pronouncing the sounds /θ/and /ð/. You have also become more aware of sentence stress and how it is used to highlight information.

1   Study the words in the box and say them aloud.

> lose   proof   surge   three   very   seem   free   theme
> loose   ferry   prove   search

a) Which words have a similar pronunciation and could be confused?

b) Can you think of any other English words that are easily confused with each other?

2   Practice saying the sentences by stressing the underlined words.

a) You can take notes <u>during</u> the lecture or <u>after</u> it.

You <u>can</u> take notes during the lecture, but you don't <u>have</u> to.

<u>You</u> can take notes during the lecture, but <u>I'm</u> not going to!

b) <u>Exports</u> rose by three percent last year, but <u>imports</u> fell.

Exports <u>rose</u> by three percent last year, after years of <u>decline</u>.

Exports rose by <u>three</u> percent last year, not the <u>eight</u> per cent reported in the media.

3   In each sentence, underline two words that you would expect to be stressed to contrast information. Practice saying the sentences with these words stressed.

a) Some species of shark attack people, but most are harmless.

b) There used to be a Chemistry Department, but it closed in 2006.

c) The aid provided to the victims was too little, too late.

d) Many banks stopped lending, when the government wanted them to lend more.

🎧 **CD1 – 46 Listen and compare your ideas with the recording.**

4   Think about what you have studied in this unit and answer the questions below.

a) Which exercises did you find most challenging?

b) Which consonant sounds do you confuse or find difficult to pronounce?

c) How is it helpful to study the phonemic symbols for different sounds?

d) Why is it helpful to be more aware of stressed words in a sentence?

> For web resources, see:
> **www.englishforacademicstudy.com/us/student/pronunciation/links**
>
> These weblinks will provide you with further practice in areas of pronunciation such as the sounds, stress, and intonation patterns of English.

Consonant Sounds 2, Word Stress on Two-Syllable Words

In this unit you will:
● learn more phonemic symbols representing consonant sounds;
● practice recognizing and producing these consonant sounds;
● learn where to place the stress in words with two syllables.

Consonant sounds

In this unit, you will focus on the consonants shaded in this table.

/p/	/t/	/k/	/s/	/ʃ/	/tʃ/	/f/	/θ/
p̲ost	t̲ake	k̲eep	s̲now	s̲hoe	c̲hoice	lea̲f	t̲hin
/b/	/d/	/g/	/z/	/ʒ/	/dʒ/	/v/	/ð/
b̲ook	d̲octor	g̲oal	z̲ero	mea̲s̲ure	j̲ump	lea̲v̲e	t̲he
/h/	/m/	/n/	/ŋ/	/l/	/r/	/w/	/ɪ/
h̲otel	m̲eet	n̲ine	bri̲ng	l̲ate	r̲ed	w̲ell	y̲es

Task 1: /ʒ/

Words ending in ~*sion* are sometimes pronounced /~ʒən/ and sometimes /~ʃən/.

1.1 🎧 **CD1 – 47 Listen to the pronunciation of the words in the box and write them under the correct heading.**

decision   version   dimension   occasion   conclusion   discussion   expression
admission   expansion   supervision   confusion   erosion

/~ʒən/	/~ʃən/

Before checking your answers, try and see a pattern in the spelling that helps you decide how ~*sion* is pronounced.

Words ending in ~*sure* are sometimes pronounced /~ʒər/, sometimes /~ʃər/ and sometimes /ʃɔːr/.

1.2   🎧 CD1 – 48 **Listen to the three different pronunciations of the word endings in the box and write them under the correct heading.**

measure   pressure   closure   assure   ensure   pleasure   leisure   exposure

/~ʒər/	/~ʃər/	/ʃɔːr/

Note: The pattern in spelling for words ending in ~*sure* is similar to that of Ex 1.1.

Words which include the letters ~*sual* also usually follow the pattern in Exs 1.1 and 1.2.

1.3   🎧 CD1 – 49 **Listen and repeat the following words.**

visual   casual   usually   sensual

Task 2: /v/

2.1   🎧 CD1 – 50 **Listen to and repeat the following words and phrases.**

| visit   develop   value   average   village   very good service |
violent   every level   voice   When does it arrive?

2.2   **Listen and repeat again, this time recording your pronunciation. Play back the recording and evaluate your pronunciation. How accurate is it?**

Pronunciation note

If you find the /v/ sound difficult to pronounce, people should still understand if you replace it with the /f/ sound (but not the /w/ sound).

So, if you can't say …   try saying …

vast	fast
view	few
invest	infest
service	surface

2.3   **If you had problems pronouncing /v/, do Ex 2.1 again, replacing /v/ with /f/.**

Task 3: /j/

3.1 CD1 – 51 The /j/ sound appears at the beginning of words starting with *y~*.
Listen and repeat.

> yet   young   yellow   year   yesterday

3.2 CD1 – 52 The /j/ sound also appears at the beginning of some words starting with *u~*. Check (✓) the words below that are pronounced /juː~/.

a) ☐ union

b) ☐ unless

c) ☐ uniform

d) ☐ uncle

e) ☐ unclear

f) ☐ unusual

g) ☐ useful

h) ☐ username

i) ☐ usual

j) ☐ uranium

k) ☐ until

l) ☐ urgent

Check your answers, listen and repeat the words.

Note: The negative forms of adjectives (e.g., *unimportant, unlikely*) are pronounced /ʌn~/.

3.3 CD1 – 53 You also find the /j/ sound in the middle of words, represented by *y*. Listen to these examples.

> beyond   layer   layout   buyer

3.4 CD1 – 54 Sometimes, the /j/ sound in the middle of words is not represented by any character. Listen to these words and mark the position of the /j/ sound in them.

Examples: contin/j/ue   comp/j/uter

a) fuel

b) view

c) argue

d) cube

e) few

f) rescue

g) distribute

Listen again and repeat the words.

Task 4: /ʃ/ and /tʃ/

4.1 ⊙ CD1 – 55 **Listen to the difference in pronunciation between these pairs of words.**

/ʃ/	/tʃ/
ship	chip
shop	chop
share	chair
shoes	choose
cash	catch
washed	watched
dishes	ditches

Listen again and repeat the words.

Pronunciation note

/ʃ/ is usually written as *sh* (*show*, *wash*).
/tʃ/ is usually written as *ch* (*cheap*, *rich*) or as *tch* (*watch*).

4.2 ⊙ CD1 – 56 **You will hear some of the words from Ex 4.1. Circle the phonemic transcription that matches the pronunciation of the word you hear.**

Example: /ʃɒp/ (/tʃɒp/)

a) /kæʃ/ /kætʃ/

b) /ʃuːz/ /tʃuːz/

c) /wɒʃd/ /wɒtʃt/

d) /ʃeər/ /tʃeər/

e) /dɪʃɪz/ /dɪtʃɪz/

f) /ʃɪp/ /tʃɪp/

4.3 Complete these sentences with words from Ex 4.1.

a) There's a small _____ on the card that stores your personal data.

b) You can pay with _____ or by check.

c) Farmers need to dig _____ to drain the soil.

d) The _____ value has shot up by 30 percent!

e) You can _____ which topic to write about for your assignment.

f) The sample should be _____ in a five percent saline solution before analysis.

4.4 🎧 CD1 – 57 **Listen to the correct answers and repeat the sentences.**

Task 5: /tʃ/ and /dʒ/

/tʃ/ is **unvoiced**, e.g., <u>ch</u>oice

/dʒ/ is **voiced**, e.g., <u>j</u>ump

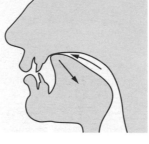

For both these sounds, the flat part of the tongue is held against the roof of the mouth. Pressure is released as you bring the tongue away from the roof of the mouth.

5.1 🎧 CD1 – 58 **Listen to the difference in pronunciation between these pairs of words.**

/tʃ/	/dʒ/
chunk	junk
cheap	Jeep
H	age
search	surge
rich	ridge
batch	badge

Listen again and repeat the words.

Pronunciation note

/dʒ/ is sometimes written as *j* (*join*, *jump*) and sometimes as *g* (*general*, *imagine*).

Note: *g* is also often pronounced /g/ (*begin*, *girl*, *give*).

5.2 🎧 CD1 – 59 **You will hear some of the words from Ex 5.1. Circle the phonemic transcription that matches the pronunciation of the word you hear.**

Example: ⟨/sɜːtʃ/⟩   /sɜːdʒ/

a)   /rɪtʃ/   /rɪdʒ/

b)   /eɪdʒ/   /eɪtʃ/

c)   /tʃʌnk/   /dʒʌnk/

d)   /bætʃ/   /bædʒ/

e)   /tʃiːp/   /dʒiːp/

5.3 **Complete these sentences with words from Ex 5.1.**

a) Most fruit and vegetables are _____ in vitamins.

b) Credit card bills are generally prepared by _____ processing of data.

c) A large _____ of the budget is spent on overheads.

d) There's a _____ of high pressure running from north-west to south-east.

e) Children today eat too much _____ food.

f) A sudden _____ in the power supply can damage your computer.

5.4 ⊙ CD1 – 60 **Listen to the correct answers and repeat the sentences.**

Task 6: Word stress on two-syllable words

6.1 ⊙ CD1 – 61 **Put the words into the correct column, according to their stress pattern.**

| provide system assist reason prepare appear |
| recent receive include certain factor question |
| problem modern suggest reduce private observe |

Example:

Oo	oO
question	provide

6.2 ⊙ CD1 – 62 **Listen to these pairs of sentences and underline the syllable that is stressed in the words in bold.**

Example:

Coffee is this country's biggest 'export.
They ex'port coffee mainly to Europe.

a) There's been a significant **increase** in unemployment.
   It's been decided to **increase** the interest rate by a quarter of a percent.

b) You need to keep a **record** of all the references you use in the essay.
   She wants to **record** the lecture with her MP3 player.

c) About 30 people were **present** at the seminar.
He plans to **present** the results of his research at the conference.

Now study the answers to Exs 6.1 and 6.2. Can you see a pattern in the pronunciation?

6.3 **Complete the explanation of the "rules" for word stress in two-syllable words, using the words in the box.**

nouns   verbs   adjectives

Most two-syllable _____ and _____ have stress on the first syllable.

Most two-syllable _____ have stress on the second syllable.

6.4 ⓐ **CD1 – 63 Unlike the two-syllable words in Ex 6.3, the stress in words ending in ~er, ~ry, ~le, ~ion, ~age, ~ish, ~ow and ~us generally falls on the first syllable. Listen and repeat these words.**

Note: The words *prefer*, *refer* and *allow* are some exceptions to this rule: they all have stress on the second syllable.

~er	~ry	~le	~ion
answer	angry	angle	action
gather	hurry	handle	mention
matter	story	middle	nation
suffer	vary	trouble	question
~age	**~ish**	**~ow**	**~us**
damage	English	follow	
language	finish	narrow	focus
manage	publish	shadow	minus
package	rubbish	window	

Unit Summary

In this unit, you have learned six English consonant sounds: /ʃ/, /tʃ/, /ʒ/, /dʒ/, /v/, /j/, and practiced their pronunciation. You have also become more aware of where to place the stress on words with two syllables.

1   **Each of the words in the box contains one of the consonant sounds in the table. Write them in the correct column below.**

> confusion   choices   unusual   average
> distribution   innovation   watched   suggest

/ʃ/	/tʃ/	/dʒ/	/z/

2   **Practice saying the words from Ex 1 and decide which words also contain other consonant sounds that you have studied in this unit (/v/ and /j/).**

3   ⦿ **CD1 – 64 Listen to the following pairs of sentences, which contain words in bold with the same spelling. Mark the stressed syllable in each pair of words. For which pairs is the word stress the same, and for which is it different?**

a)   The **contracts** were signed last week.
        The metal **contracts** as it cools down.

b)   It caused a lot of **damage**.
        How does it **damage** your health?

c)   Why did they **object** to the proposal?
        Archaeologists aren't sure what this **object** was used for.

d)   What's the main **focus** of your research?
        We need to **focus** on the real issues.

> For web resources, see:
> **www.englishforacademicstudy.com/us/student/pronunciation/links**
>
> These weblinks will provide you with further practice in areas of pronunciation such as the sounds, stress, and intonation patterns of English.

Diphthongs 1, Sounds in Connected Speech

In this unit you will:
- learn which phonemic symbols represent certain diphthongs;
- practice recognizing and producing diphthongs;
- learn how the pronunciation of words is affected by their context in connected speech.

Diphthongs

Diphthongs can be thought of as combinations of two vowels. For example, the /eɪ/ sound in *day* starts as /e/ and then ends /ɪ/.

In this unit, you will focus on the diphthongs shaded in this table.

/aɪ/	/aʊ/	/oʊ/	/eɪ/	/eə/	/ɪə/	/ɔɪ/	/ʊə/
why	n<u>ow</u>	g<u>o</u>	d<u>ay</u>	c<u>are</u>	d<u>ear</u>	enj<u>oy</u>	p<u>ure</u>

Task 1: /aɪ/ and /ɪ/

1.1 🎧 CD2 – 1 **Put the words in the box into the correct column, according to the pronunciation of the vowel or diphthong sound.**

time	think	life	write	while	win	high
try	sit	site	buy	bit	might	sign	like

/aɪ/	/ɪ/

Pronunciation note

(**C** = consonant)

The /aɪ/ sound often occurs in:

- one-syllable words ending ~i**C**e: *fine*, *rise*, *drive*;
- words including **C**igh: *light*, *fight*, *thigh*;
- one-syllable words written **CC**y: *why*, *sky*, *dry*.

The /ɪ/ sound:

- is often written **C**i**C**: *lid*, *fit*, *ship*;
- often occurs in unstressed syllables: *décide*, *mínute (n)*.

However, there are exceptions to these patterns, e.g., *give*, *live (v)*.

1.2 **Make sure your answers to Ex 1.1 fit these patterns.**

1.3 **CD2 – 2 How do you pronounce *L-I-V-E* in each of these sentences?**

   a) Where do you live?

   b) The match is being shown live on TV.

   Why is the pronunciation different in each sentence?

1.4 **CD2 – 3 Listen to the six words below and complete the two activities.**

   a) Circle the phonemic transcription that matches the pronunciation of the word you hear.

   1 /wɪl/ _____   /waɪl/ _____
   2 /fɪt/ _____   /faɪt/ _____
   3 /stɪl/ _____   /staɪl/ _____
   4 /hɪt/ _____   /haɪt/ _____
   5 /lɪtər/ _____   /laɪtər/ _____
   6 /hɪd/ _____   /haɪd/ _____

   b) Now write the words, with the correct spelling, in the spaces next to the phonemic transcriptions.

1.5 **CD2 – 4 Underline the /aɪ/ sounds in these sentences or phrases. Then listen and repeat them.**

   a) Try the other side.
   b) The height's fine.
   c) This type of plant needs a lot of light.
   d) There was a slight rise in the share value.

Task 2: /oʊ/ and /ɒ/

2.1 🎧 **CD2 – 5 Put the words in the box into the correct column, according to the pronunciation of the vowel or diphthong sound.**

| cost coast show rod road grow lot load |
| flow hope code cold not note fold |

/oʊ/	/ɒ/

Pronunciation note

(**C** = consonant)

The /oʊ/ sound often occurs in:

- one-syllable words ending ~o**C**e: *drove, hole, tone;*
- words including *oa*: *loan, float, coat;*
- words ending ~*ow*: *throw, slow, below.*

The /ɒ/ sound:

- is often written **C**o**C**: *got, sock, shop;*
- is sometimes written *a*: *what, wash, want.*

However, there are exceptions to these patterns.

- *more, some, gone*
- *board, abroad, coarse*
- *now, how*

2.2 **Make sure your answers to Ex 2.1 fit these patterns.**

2.3 🎧 CD2 – 6 **Listen to the six words below and complete the activities.**

a) Listen and circle the phonemic transcription that matches the pronunciation of the word you hear.

1 /kɒst/ _____ /koʊst/ _____

2 /nɒt/ _____ /noʊt/ _____

3 /rɒd/ _____ /roʊd/ _____

4 /sɒk/ _____ /soʊk/ _____

5 /wɒnt/ _____ /woʊnt/ _____

6 /fɒnd/ _____ /foʊnd/ _____

b) Write the words, with the correct spelling, in the spaces next to the phonemic transcriptions.

2.4 🎧 CD2 – 7 **Underline the /oʊ/ sounds in these sentences or phrases. Then listen and repeat.**

a) Most of the gold is exported.

b) … the hole in the ozone layer …

c) Gross profits were down.

d) Can you cope with the workload?

Task 3: /eɪ/, /æ/ and /ɑː/

3.1 🎧 CD2 – 8 **Put the words in the box into the correct column, according to the pronunciation of the vowel or diphthong sound.**

| plan plane dark face make scale large lack |
| heart play weigh gain part claim bad |

/eɪ/	/æ/	/ɑː/

Pronunciation note

(**C** = consonant)

The /eɪ/ sound often occurs in:

- one-syllable words ending ~a**C**e: *place, rate, save*;
- words ending ~ay: *away, stay, today*;
- one-syllable words with *ai*: *paint, raise, train*.

The /ɑː/ sound is often found in words with *ar*, but the *r* is often silent in British English: *far, start, hard*.

However, there are exceptions to these patterns, e.g., *have, care*.

3.2 Make sure your answers to Ex 3.1 fit these patterns.

3.3 CD2 – 9 Listen to the eight words below and complete the activities.

a) Circle the phonemic transcription that matches the pronunciation of the word you hear.

1 /læk/ _____   /leɪk/ _____
2 /tæp/ _____   /teɪp/ _____
3 /plæn/ _____   /pleɪn/ _____
4 /lætər/ _____   /leɪtər/ _____
5 /ɑːrm/ _____   /eɪm/ _____
6 /mɑːrk/ _____   /meɪk/ _____
7 /pɑːs/ _____   /peɪs/ _____
8 /kɑːm/ _____   /keɪm/ _____

b) Now write the words, with the correct spelling, in the spaces next to the phonemic transcriptions.

3.4 CD2 – 10 Underline the /eɪ/ sounds in these sentences or phrases. Then listen and repeat.

a) Can you explain this heavy rainfall?

b) That's quite a claim to make.

c) The future remains uncertain.

d) The failure rate is quite high.

Task 4: Sounds in connected speech

4.1 CD2 – 11 **Listen to these short conversations.**

a) What do we need to solve the problem? A system.

b) What would you like me to do? Assist him.

In the two conversations, each response sounds almost identical. When you are talking, the pronunciation of some words is affected by the words before or after them.

- Words may seem to be *joined* together (linking).

- A sound may be *inserted* between words.

- A sound may *disappear* or be very difficult to hear.

- A sound may *change*.

Linking: Consonant + vowel

4.2 CD2 – 12 **Listen to the following examples.**

hand‿in

split‿up

complex‿issue

When a word ends in a consonant sound and the next word begins with a vowel sound, the words may seem to be linked.

4.3 CD2 – 13 **Listen to these phrases and repeat them, linking the words together where this is indicated.**

a) divide‿in two

b) historical‿evidence

c) as soon‿as possible

d) take‿over control

e) it'll‿end next week

f) the Data Protection‿Act

g) a wide‿area

h) keep‿up with‿it

i) an‿increase‿in crime

j) the main‿aim

4.4 🎧 CD2 – 14 **Listen to this introduction from a talk about home ownership and write in the links between words.**

> In this presentation I'm going to talk about home ownership in the UK. First I'm going to focus on changes in the patterns of home ownership in the last 20 years and provide an explanation for these changes. Then I'm going to describe the process of buying or selling a house. Finally I'm going to try to make some predictions about the housing market.

4.5 **Listen again and repeat the text in sections. Try to link words where this is appropriate.**

Inserting sounds between words: Vowel (V) + vowel

4.6 🎧 CD2 – 15 **Listen to the following examples.**

…V/ʷ/V…

slow/ʷ/economic growth

true/ʷ/identity

go/ʷ/up

Where a word ends with a vowel and the next word starts with a vowel, it is often easier to pronounce if we insert /w/, /ʝ/ or /r/ between the vowels.

If the first word ends in a vowel pronounced with *rounded lips*, we often insert a /w/ sound. In the written form, the first word may end in *w*.

Listen again and see if you can produce the /w/ sound.

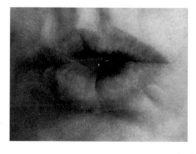

4.7 🎧 CD2 – 16 **Listen to the following examples.**

…V/ʝ/V…

carry/ʝ/on

high/ʝ/altitude

free/ʝ/access

If the first word ends in a vowel pronounced with *stretched lips*, we often insert a /ʝ/ sound. In the written form, the first word may end in *y*.

Listen again and see if you can produce the /ʝ/ sound.

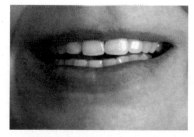

4.8   🎧 CD2 – 17 **Listen to the following examples.**

...V/r/V...

aware/r/of the problem

after/r/all

faster/r/access

If the first word ends in the /ə/ sound, we often insert the /r/ sound. In the written form, the first word may end in ~re, ~er or ~or.

Listen again and see if you can produce the /r/ sound.

Note: Most speakers of British English do not pronounce the r at the ends of words unless the word is followed by a vowel. However, many speakers of other Englishes, for example American English, *do* pronounce the r in most contexts.

4.9   🎧 CD2 – 18 **Listen to these phrases and decide if a /w/, /j/ or /r/ sound needs to be inserted.**

a) try out

b) agree on this

c) two of them

d) driver error

e) radio operator

f) high above the Earth

g) How does this tie in?

4.10 **Listen again and repeat the phrases, inserting the sounds where appropriate.**

Unit Summary

In this unit, you have learned the phonemic symbols for the diphthongs /aɪ/, /oʊ/ and /eɪ/ and looked at sound/spelling patterns for words that contain them. You have also become more aware of how the pronunciation of words is affected by their context in connected speech.

1 🎧 **CD2 – 19 Underline the diphthong sounds /aɪ/ in sentence (a), /oʊ/ in sentence (b) and /eɪ/ in sentence (c).**

a) I think I'd like to carry on with Life Sciences, but I'm also interested in Psychology.

b) I want to go into social work, so I'm studying Sociology.

c) He came to Boston to present a paper on International Relations.

2 **Identify the words in the sentences in Ex 1 that would normally be linked. Draw in the links like this:**

I‿think‿I'd like to‿carry …

Listen again and make sure your answers are correct.

3 **Study the words below; they are all from the sentences in Ex 1. Which sounds are normally inserted between them to make them easier to pronounce in connected speech?**

a) carry on

b) go into

c) paper on

4 **Practice saying the sentences aloud, using the connected speech features you have looked at in the unit.**

5 **Think about the statements below. Do you agree or disagree with them?**

a) It is more important to be able to hear the difference between English vowel sounds and diphthongs than to be able to produce them all correctly.

b) Students need to be able to understand how English speakers link sounds and words together, but don't need to speak in the same way themselves.

For web resources, see:

www.englishforacademicstudy.com/us/student/pronunciation/links

These weblinks will provide you with further practice in areas of pronunciation such as the sounds, stress, and intonation patterns of English.

6

Consonant Clusters 1, Tone Units 1

In this unit you will:
- learn how to pronounce groups of consonants (consonant clusters) at the beginning and in the middle of words;
- learn how to divide up connected speech into tone units.

Consonant clusters

In English, you may find groups of two or three consonant sounds:

- at the beginning of words: *grow, square, straight*;
- in the middle of words: *computer, expression, congratulate*;
- at the end of words: *hoped, branch, strength*;
- across two words: *room number, clamp down*.

In other languages, there may be a tendency for the pattern to be consonant – vowel – consonant – vowel, and speakers of such languages may find it difficult to pronounce certain consonant clusters.

Task 1: Consonant clusters at the beginning of words

1.1 🎧 **CD2 – 20 Listen and repeat these groups of words, which begin with consonant clusters.**

blame	platform	claim	glass	flexible
blind	plenty	climate	global	flight
blood	plus	closure	glue	flow
brand	practice	create	graphics	fraction
break	pressure	crucial	ground	freeze
brief	profit	criteria	growth	frequent
draw	transaction	quarter	twelve	threat
draft	trend	quality	twice	through
drop	trigger	quota	twin	throw
				shrink
				shred

Note which of these consonant clusters you have problems pronouncing and try to focus on these in future practice.

1.2 🎧 **CD2 – 21 Listen and complete these sentences.**

The missing words all begin with a consonant cluster.

a) It burns with a blue _____.

b) There was a _____ rise in crime.

c) We are on _____ for ten percent _____ this year.

d) We need a more _____ definition of the term.

e) It's covered with a steel _____.

f) The _____ needs to be replaced.

g) Its development can be _____ back to the 15th century.

h) The screen went _____.

i) There's _____ evidence for such a link.

j) It's difficult to follow the _____ of his argument.

1.3 **Listen again and repeat the phrases. Try to focus on the correct pronunciation of the consonant cluster, on the correct word stress, and on linking.**

1.4 🎧 **CD2 – 22 Listen and repeat these further examples of consonant clusters that begin with /s/.**

scale	sleep	spare	split	straight
scheme	slip	spill	splendid	stress
scope	slight	speed	stage	strike
score	slope	spoil	step	strong
screen	smart	specific	store	sweet
script	smell	spray	stuff	swing
snack	smoke	spread	style	switch
snow	smooth	spring		

1.5 🎧 **CD2 – 23 Listen and complete these phrases or sentences.**

The missing words all begin with /s/ and a consonant cluster.

a) This machine _____ the brain.

b) Resources are _____.

c) This _____ is under threat.

d) We're making _____ progress.

e) one important _____

f) He _____ paint on the floor.

g) a _____ feeling

h) a bigger _____ of the cake

i) in a _____ condition

j) a _____ floor

1.6 **Listen again and repeat the phrases or sentences. Try to focus on the correct pronunciation of the consonant cluster, on the correct word stress, and on linking.**

Task 2: Consonant clusters in the middle of words

2.1 🎧 CD2 – 24 **Listen and repeat these words, which include consonant clusters.**

impress	central	explain	include	abstract
comprise	contract	exploit	conclude	construct
compromise	control	explore	enclose	distribute
	entry	explicit	unclear	industry
complain	introduce			illustrate
complete		extract	conflict	
employ	inspect	extreme	influence	
sample	transport		inflation	

2.2 🎧 CD2 – 25 **Listen and complete these phrases or sentences with words from Ex 2.1.**

a) Supplies need to be _____.

b) no _____ reference

c) the _____ infrastructure

d) this _____ with

e) The causes are _____.

f) oils _____ from plants

g) an _____ concept

h) in order to _____ its potential fully

i) It _____ three parts.

j) in _____ cases

2.3 **Listen again and repeat the phrases or sentences. Try to focus on the correct pronunciation of the consonant cluster, on the correct word stress, and on linking.**

Task 3: Disappearing sounds in connected speech

3.1 🎧 CD2 – 26 **Listen to these sentences and write in the word that is missing.**

a) Did _____ tell you?

b) I've added _____ name to the list.

c) Can you put _____ suitcase in the car?

When function words beginning with *h*, like *he, his, him, her*, are *unstressed* and in the *middle* of a sentence, the /h/ sound often disappears.

However, if these words are at the *beginning* of a sentence, the /h/ sound is usually pronounced, e.g., *He left at four o'clock*.

Contractions of auxiliary and modal verbs

In connected speech, auxiliary verbs and some modal verbs are often contracted; that is to say, some of the sounds disappear when they are unstressed. Here is a list of some of the most common contractions.

Full form	Contraction	Full form	Contraction
he is / he has she is / she has they are they have	he's she's they're they've	could have should have must have	could've should've must've
it would / it had he would / he had	it'd he'd	is not are not will not can not would not	isn't aren't won't can't wouldn't

Note:
1 In academic writing, you should use the full forms and not the contracted forms.
2 *he's* might represent *he is* or *he has,* depending on context.
3 *he'd* might represent *he had* or *he would,* depending on context.

3.2 🔊 CD2 – 27 **Listen and complete the sentences.**

Note: There are two or three words missing from each space.

a) Although _____ requested further funding, _____ not certain that the project will continue beyond 2015.

b) The treatment is expensive, and _____ why _____ not very widely available.

c) Another advantage is that _____ lower the costs.

d) In fact, _____ supposed to be checked every six months.

e) We _____ know for sure, but _____ thought that the space probe _____ been hit by a meteorite.

f) Unfortunately, _____ forgotten just how complicated the process is.

g) The Vikings are believed _____ landed in America well before Columbus.

h) The equipment testing _____ been left until the last minute.

3.3 🔊 CD2 – 28 **Listen to these words and phrases and, in the words in bold, cross out the vowels that are not pronounced.**

Note: Unstressed short vowels in some words sometimes disappear, too.

Example: *comfortable* is often pronounced /ˈkʌmftəbəl/, so the letters ~or~ are not pronounced.

a) **Vegetables** are grown on about 60 percent of farms in the area.

b) **Perhaps** he's left.

c) The **laboratory** is closed on Sundays.

d) I'll **probably** be late.

e) He lives a **comfortable** life.

3.4 🎧 **CD2 – 29 Listen to the sentences a–e, paying particular attention to the consonant clusters in the words in bold. Cross out the consonants that are not pronounced.**

Where you have groups of consonants together (consonant clusters), some consonants may disappear to make them easier to pronounce in normal informal speech.

Example: *next month* is pronounced /neks mʌnθ/, so the letter *t* may disappear.

a) It **reacts** with sulphur.

b) They'll **send** back the results on Tuesday.

c) It **must** be checked.

d) The low election turnout **reflects** growing apathy towards politics.

e) The engine **tends** to overheat in particular circumstances.

Generally, as in the above examples, the consonants *t* and *d* are only dropped when they are trapped between other consonants, rather than vowels.

Task 4: Tone units

Whereas written English is split into words, spoken English is split into what are known as tone units. Each tone unit contains at least one prominent syllable. If, however, it contains two, then it is usually the second that contains the main sentence stress. This is the tonic syllable, and it is where most of the pitch change takes place.

4.1 🎧 **CD2 – 30 Listen to someone speaking the above text and notice how it is split into tone units.**

Whereas **writ**ten **Eng**lish // is split into **words** // **spok**en English // is **split** into what are **known** // as **tone** units //. Each **tone un**it // contains at least one **prom**inent **syll**able //. If, how**ev**er, // it contains **two** //, then it's **u**sually the **se**cond // which contains the **main** sentence **stress** //. This is the **ton**ic **syll**able // and it is where **most** of the **pitch change** // **takes place** //.

4.2 🎧 **CD2 – 31 Listen to part of the lecture entitled *An Introduction to British Agriculture*. Mark the tone units by writing in double slash signs (//) in the right places.**

You will find it helpful to listen for brief pauses and changes in speaker key.

As a backdrop to all these activities, particularly after the Second World War, a lot of effort was put into research and development of agriculture in terms of plant breeding, breeding crops that were higher yielding, that were perhaps disease-resistant, and so on and so forth. Also, crops that might have better quality, better bread-making quality, higher gluten content to make them doughy, higher protein content, and so on and so forth. Research, too, and this is again at one of the university farms, research into livestock production. Understanding how to better manage our livestock, again to make them produce more, certainly, but also to produce and influence the quality of the livestock products, whether that happens to be milk or cheese, come back to that in a moment, or indeed meat.

⊕ **CD2 – 32 Now listen to an extract from the lecture on globalization. Mark the tone units by writing in double slash signs (//) in the right places.**

Now to get to the meat of the lecture, the basic purpose of this lecture is to give you some overview of the kind of contemporary academic and policy debate about globalization and particularly about a very specific, although rather general debate itself, that's the debate on the effect of globalization on the role of the state. So you see on the overhead the lecture's going to be kind of in two parts: the first will be looking at globalization, causes and consequences and more particularly a kind of definition of the discussion of some of the competing concepts of globalization, that is, y'know, what people say it is, so that we can then discuss in some detail hopefully this question of how globalization is affecting the state.

Unit Summary

In this unit, you have focused on the correct pronunciation of consonant clusters at the beginning and in the middle of words. You have also looked at sounds that disappear in connected speech and have become more aware of how English speech is divided into tone units.

1   🎧 **CD2 – 33 Listen to how the following words are pronounced. Say the words in each group below. Underline any words that you find difficult to pronounce.**

a) spare	spoil	speed	spray
b) central	entry	quarter	track
c) school	scale	share	scheme
d) street	store	stress	straight
e) complete	complex	construct	comprise
f) abstract	industry	construct	inspect

2   **Identify the consonant cluster in each word.**

3   **Decide which word you think is the odd one out in each group.**

Note: There may be more than one possible answer.

4   **Read the text and then answer the questions below.**

You've got some interesting ideas and make some good points, but you could have developed these a little more. You must make sure that you go through your essay for spelling mistakes and make sure the grammar is correct. Perhaps you should've asked the graduate assistant to read through your work. He would have helped you improve it.

a)   🎧 **CD2 – 34** Listen to someone speaking the above text and mark the tone units.

b)   Try to read the text aloud as you listen to the recording, paying attention to the consonant clusters and tone units.

For web resources, see:

www.englishforacademicstudy.com/us/student/pronunciation/links

These weblinks will provide you with further practice in areas of pronunciation such as the sounds, stress, and intonation patterns of English.

7 Diphthongs 2, Tone Units 2

In this unit you will:
- learn which phonemic symbols represent other diphthongs;
- practice recognizing and producing these diphthongs;
- have more practice identifying sentence stress and tone units.

Diphthongs

In this unit, you will focus on the diphthongs shaded in this table.

/aɪ/	/aʊ/	/oʊ/	/eɪ/	/eə/	/ɪə/	/ɔɪ/	/ʊə/
wh<u>y</u>	n<u>ow</u>	g<u>o</u>	d<u>ay</u>	<u>c</u>are	d<u>ear</u>	enj<u>oy</u>	p<u>ure</u>

Task 1: /eə/ and /ɪə/

1.1 🎧 CD2 – 35 **Put the words in the box into the correct column of the table, according to the pronunciation of the diphthong sound.**

> share   fair   mere   square   near   adhere   sphere   year   there   where
>
> aware   appear   severe   wear   pair   chair   bear   fare

/eə/	/ɪə/

Pronunciation note

The /eə/ sound often occurs in words ending with:

- ~are: care, prepare;
- ~air: hair, repair.

The /ɪə/ sound often occurs in words ending with:

- ~ear: fear, gear;
- ~ere: here, sincere.

However, there are exceptions to these patterns, e.g., wear /weə/, bear /beə/, where /weə/ and there /ðeə/.

1.2   **Make sure your answers to Ex 1.1 fit these patterns.**

1.3   ⊕ CD2 – 36 **Using words from Ex 1.1, complete these sentences by writing in the missing words.**

    a) As far as I'm _____, there's been little previous research into this issue.

    b) Patients suffering from _____ depression are often treated with drugs.

    c) The _____ fact that they have agreed to negotiate does not indicate that an end to the conflict is near.

    d) These countries needed to _____ for entry into the EMU.

    e) How can we _____ the damage that has been done?

    f) The area of land is about 20 _____ meters.

    g) The seeds _____ to the fur of animals, which distribute them over a large area.

    h) We need to _____ in mind that events in South America are largely beyond the UK's _____ of influence.

Listen again and repeat.

Task 2: /aʊ/ and /oʊ/

2.1   ⊕ CD2 – 37 **Put the words in the box into the correct column of the table, according to the pronunciation of *ow*.**

| allow   crowd   below   own   flow   down   power   growth   now   know |
| slow   follow   brown   show   powder   crown   owe   shower |

/aʊ/	/oʊ/

Note: The letters *ow* are sometimes pronounced /aʊ/ and sometimes /oʊ/.

2.2 ⊙ CD2 – 38 **Underline the words below which include the /aʊ/ sound.**

Note: The letters *ou* are often also pronounced /aʊ/, but not always.

loud	doubt	group	account	court	serious	sound	various	trouble	
south	amount	color	course	enough	young	hour	ground	flavor	

2.3 ⊙ CD2 – 39 **Listen and complete the sentences, using words from Exs 2.1 and 2.2.**

a) How do we _____ for this increase in temperature?

b) Margaret Thatcher came to _____ in 1979.

c) The new road system is designed to improve traffic _____ through the city center.

d) The animal feed is usually sold in _____ form.

e) It's without _____ the most _____ crisis the government has faced.

f) You need to _____ 21 days for delivery.

g) Economic _____ has slowed down over the last six months.

h) He's doing research into _____ behavior.

i) A significant _____ of water is lost through perspiration.

j) The cheese has quite a strong _____ .

Listen again and repeat.

Task 3: /ɔɪ/

3.1 ⊙ CD2 – 40 **Listen and repeat the following words.**

Note: The letters *oi* and *oy* are usually pronounced /ɔɪ/.

coin	point	join	avoid	soil	noise
boy	employ	enjoy	royal	annoy	soy

3.2 ⊙ CD2 – 41 **Listen and complete these sentences by writing a word in each space.**

Note: Each word includes the letters *oi* or *oy*, but they are not words from the previous exercise.

a) The questionnaire comprises multiple-_____ and open questions.

b) The government wants parents to have a _____ in determining how their children are educated.

c) During the civil war, the army remained _____ to the king.

d) The company has _____ a new marketing director.

e) Large parts of the city were _____ in the earthquake.

f) It's often claimed that we fail to _____ scientific developments made in UK universities.

g) Many sailors died during long sea _____ because of poor nutrition.

h) The new company is a _____ venture between Italian and Egyptian _____ companies.

Listen again and repeat.

Task 4: Tone units 2

4.1 **CD2 – 42 Listen and complete this lecture on higher education in the US. Write one to five words in each space.**

... in the US, _____ do that _____
to tell you something about the education _____ before students
_____ level. There are _____ reasons for this.
_____ it's part of the plan of your course _____
to give you the experience of lectures before you go into your real departments in
September, _____ is that we've found _____
_____ that many students come to the US and they live and study here _____
_____ and they go away without knowing _____
most basic facts about the education system here. It's _____ that the
education system here, _____ your countries, is changing very rapidly,
and this means _____ people, you know, people as old as me, who
don't _____ have direct _____, they probably
give you information about the education system as _____ rather
than as it _____ is now.

Now what qualifications, _____, do I have to speak on this particular
_____? Well, I'm, _____ in the introduction, I'm
here at Boston University and my main _____ is to look after
international students here, like you, who need academic language support. Now between
20 and 23 percent of the students in this university, in Boston University, don't have English
as their first language and didn't receive their previous education in the United States.
So that's a large number of students, _____ almost two thousand five
hundred students, in this university who were not _____ educated
in the United States before they came to the university, so you are among many.
_____ a minority, but you're a very large minority.

4.2 **Listen again and mark the tone units in Ex 4.1 by writing in double slash signs (//) in the right places. Look back to Unit 6, Task 4, for an explanation of tone units.**

4.3 ⊙ CD2 – 43 Listen to this excerpt from a lecture titled *Financial Markets and Instruments* and decide where the sentence stress falls.

> Well, the title, *Financial Markets and Instruments*, what are we going to do here? Well, we're going to start by explaining why we need a financial market at all. What's the role that is played by a financial market? What's the rationale for having a financial market? And then we're going to move on and explain some of the instruments that are traded in those markets, some of the instruments that I was saying you're familiar with already, because they are simply stocks, bonds, bills: money market instruments. If you've taken any finance courses before, you might be familiar also with the other ones, which are future swap options, which are derivative instruments, and I'm going to focus mainly on the stocks, bonds, bills, since these are by far the easiest to understand. OK, let's start with a simple definition, and I guess anyone here could have given this definition on their own: what's a financial market? Well, a financial market is a market where financial securities are traded. Nothing very tricky here.

4.4 Listen again and mark the tone units in Ex 4.3 by writing in double slash signs (//) in the right places.

Unit Summary

In this unit, you have learned the phonemic symbols for the diphthongs /eə/, /ɪə/, /aʊ/ and /ɔɪ/ and looked at sound/spelling patterns for words that contain them. You have also had more practice in identifying sentence stress and tone units.

1   **Each of the words in the box contains one of the diphthongs in the table below. Write them in the correct column.**

annoy	square	crowd	growth	severe	soy	although	doubt
steer	owe	pair	south	bear ·	avoid	year	

eə	ɪə	aʊ	oʊ	ɔɪ

🔊 **CD2 – 44 Listen and check your answers.**

2   **Write three more words for each column. Choose words from the unit or from your area of study.**

3   **Study the different spelling patterns for each sound. Are there any exceptions to the patterns that you looked at in the unit?**

4   **Read the statements below and decide whether you agree with each one or not.**

a) English words can be hard to pronounce because there are so many vowel sounds and spelling patterns.

b) Looking at the phonemes for the vowel or diphthong sounds in a new word helps me remember its pronunciation.

c) It is important to understand how native speakers join words together and omit sounds when they speak in English.

d) It is less important for non-native speakers to use connected speech features themselves.

e) It is easier to understand a talk or lecture if you are aware of how the speaker divides his or her speech into tone units.

For web resources, see:

www.englishforacademicstudy.com/us/student/pronunciation/links

These weblinks will provide you with further practice in areas of pronunciation such as the sounds, stress, and intonation patterns of English.

8 Consonant Clusters 2, Intonation

In this unit you will:
● learn how to pronounce consonant clusters at the end of words and across two words;
● learn how intonation is used to organize and emphasize information.

Task 1: Consonant clusters

In Unit 6, you studied consonant clusters at the beginning and in the middle of words. In this unit, you will learn how to pronounce consonant clusters at the end of words and across two words.

1.1 ● CD2 – 45 **Listen and repeat these groups of words, which end with consonant clusters.**

Note: In some cases, you may hear a very short /ə/ between the consonants. A word like *arrival* may be pronounced as /əˈraɪvl/ or as /əˈraɪvəl/.

arrival	impact	criticism	depth	branch
critical	conflict	mechanism	length	lunch
external	affect	organism	strength	launch
financial	abstract	tourism	width	bench
principal			wealth	
	range	eleven		
assemble	arrange	given		
resemble	change	govern		
	challenge	driven		

1.2 ● CD2 – 46 **Listen to these phrases and sentences and write the missing words in the spaces.**

Note: All the words end in consonant clusters.

a) in the _____ stage

b) The job has some _____ benefits.

c) I've lost a _____ of keys.

d) a rather _____ surface

e) It was discussed at some _____.

f) This is a key _____ of his work.

g) He's studying _____ at Leeds University.

h) They can't afford to take such a _____.

i) the _____ of investment controls

j) in the _____ grade

1.3 🎧 CD2 – 47 **Listen to the past verb forms in the box and put them in the correct column of the table, depending on the pronunciation of ~ed.**

Note: Simple past and past participle forms of regular verbs are formed by adding ~*ed*, and this ending is pronounced /t/, /d/ or /ɪd/, depending on the verb.

equipped	combined	involved	concluded	constructed
depended	developed	expressed	claimed	advised	arranged
adapted	lacked	finished	absorbed

/t/ or /d/	/ɪd/

Pronunciation note

When the infinitive form ends in /t/ or /d/, you add /ɪd/.

Examples:

want	⟶	wanted
vote	⟶	voted
avoid	⟶	avoided
decide	⟶	decided

When the infinitive ends with any other *unvoiced* consonant, you add /t/.

Examples:

stop	⟶	stopped
pick	⟶	picked
push	⟶	pushed

When the infinitive ends with any other *voiced* consonant, a vowel or a diphthong, you add /d/.

Examples:

try	⟶	tried
tag	⟶	tagged
tamper	⟶	tampered

In Unit 6, Ex 3.4, we listened to examples of how the consonants *t* and *d* are dropped when they are trapped between other consonants. Sometimes, dropping *t* and *d* can eliminate the distinction between present simple and past simple verb forms, which means that the examples in Ex 1.4 are likely to sound the same.

1.4   ⓟ CD2 – 48 **Listen to the following examples.**

I watch television every night.

and

I watched television last night.

or

Many suppliers raise their prices in situations like this.

and

Many suppliers raised their prices when the exchange rate rose.

These examples show that, when listening, you need to compare what you hear with your understanding of the context, to make sure that you correctly decode meaning.

> ## Pronunciation note
>
> If you find it difficult to pronounce the consonant clusters, try imagining that the final consonant is part of the following word.
>
> For example, if you find it difficult to say *It lacked a clear focus*, try saying *It lack ta clear focus*.

1.5   ⓟ CD2 – 49 **Listen and repeat these phrases.**

a) arranged at short notice

b) the team involved in the project

c) it was constructed in three months

d) it's absorbed into the bloodstream

e) the benefits claimed in the report

f) we've avoided the problem

g) a technique developed in Brazil

h) specially adapted equipment

i) aimed at a niche market

j) enclosed in plastic

Task 2: Intonation

2.1   ⓟ CD2 – 50 **Listen to the following short exchange.**

A: Has everything been checked?

B: Yes, I think so.

A: What about the ↓temperature?

B: Yes, I've checked the ↑temperature, and it's normal.

In the last two lines, the word *temperature* is stressed. However, if you listen carefully, you will hear that the voice goes down in tone in the first instance (*falling intonation*) and up in tone in the second instance (*rising intonation*).

Listen to the two words in isolation.

A: ↓temperature

B: ↑temperature

2.2 🎧 CD2 – 51 **Listen to another short exchange and do the three activities below.**

A: It's too expensive.

B: Well, it's expensive, but it's worth it.

a) Underline the word that is stressed in each sentence.

b) Note whether there is a rising (↑) or falling (↓) intonation on the stressed words.

c) Listen again and check your answers.

Pronunciation note

In English, speakers use intonation for different functions. The main ones come under these two categories:

- to organize and emphasize information;
- to show their attitude to the topic under discussion.

Like sentence stress, changes of intonation are affected by speaker choice and context. They are not governed by a clear set of rules.

In the exchanges in Exs 2.1 and 2.2, the reasons for the choice of intonation patterns are as follows:

- a *falling tone*, e.g., ↓*temperature*, is generally used when the speaker *introduces a new idea into the discussion*;
- a *rising tone*, e.g., ↑*temperature*, is generally used when the speaker *refers to an idea that has already been introduced*. In other words, it is <u>not</u> a new idea in the discussion.

A falling intonation is generally used when a conclusion has been reached.

In sentence 4 of Ex 2.1 ,this occurs on the word *normal*, which therefore has a falling tone: *I've checked the ↑temperature, and it's ↓normal.*

2.3 🎧 CD2 – 52 **Compare this conversation with the previous one.**

Note: Even when we use different words to refer back to a previous idea, there is still a rising intonation.

A: It's too ↓**expensive**.

B: Yes, it's a lot of ↑**money**, but it's ↓worth it.

In this case, *money* has a rising tone because it refers back to the idea of *expensive*.

Speaking & Pronunciation

2.4 ⊙ CD2 – 53 **Listen to these short conversations. Notice the falling intonation for new information and the rising tone for information that is not new.**

a) **A:** When's the ↓**deadline** for the new building project?

   B: The ↑**deadline**? I think it's next Thursday.

b) **A:** Why do these prices ↓**fluctuate**?

   B: Changes in the exchange rate cause this ↑**variation**.

2.5 ⊙ CD2 – 54 **Listen to this conversation and mark the falling and rising intonation.**

Note: The rise or fall starts on the stressed word and continues to the end of the tone unit (see page 185). The first rise has been marked for you as an example. The stressed words are in bold.

A: Can I ↑**help** you?

B: Yes, where's the **Physics** Department?

A: It's on the second **floor**.

B: On the **second** floor?

A: Yes, that's right. Take the **elevator** over there.

B: I don't like **elevators**. I'd rather **walk** there.

A: Suit yourself. The **stairs** are down the **hall**, on the **left**.

B: **Down there**, on the **left**. Thanks very much!

2.6 **Now take the role of Student B and reply to Student A in the pauses provided.**

2.7 ⊙ CD2 – 55 **Listen to this short extract from a lecture and think about the use of intonation.**

> In these two lectures, we're going to look at two theories of child **development**. First, I'm going to look at Jean **Piaget**. Then, next week, I'll talk about the life and work of Erick **Erickson**. So this week, it's about Jean **Piaget**. Now Piaget's theories were very much influenced by his own experiences, so I'm going to talk about his life and how he developed his ideas, and then I'm going to describe Piaget's four stages of child **development**.

2.8 **What is the speaker signaling by his use of falling intonation on the words in bold?**

Note: When we are listening to lectures, we need to understand how the speaker signals what he is going to say through his use of intonation.

2.9 ⊚ CD2 – 56 **Listen to a student talking about the advantages and disadvantages of streaming video from a website and mark the rising and falling tones on the stressed words in bold.**

> With **streaming** video, the video is **downloaded** to your **computer** as you are **listening** to it. And usually you can't **save** it.
>
> This **stops** people from making **copies** of the video, **editing** or **pirating** it.
>
> The **problem** is, if you don't have enough **bandwidth**, or if you're on a **network** and it's very **busy**, your **computer** won't be able to download **fast** enough.
>
> As a **result**, the picture quality is often **poor**, or the pictures are **jerky**. Sometimes, the video even **freezes**.

2.10 **Think about the use of falling and rising tones in the previous audio extracts. Did a falling tone signal the speaker was introducing a new idea and a rising tone signal the speaker was referring to an idea that had already been introduced, as suggested in the previous Pronunciation note?**

If you were listening carefully, you may have picked up examples of a more subtle phenomenon, the fall–rise, used where there is no back reference, e.g., *first* or *next week*.

2.11 **Listen again to Tracks 55 and 56. Can you recall any other examples?**

2.12 ⊚ CD2 – 57 **Listen again to the first dialogue in Ex 2.1.**

As mentioned in the previous note, intonation, or tone of voice, is also used to show the speaker's attitude. It is for this purpose that the fall–rise is most often employed. If you were listening carefully, you may have picked this up already.

A: Has everything been ↓↑checked? (conveying concern)

B: Yes, I ↓↑think so. (But I'm not sure—conveying uncertainty.)

Consider also:

A: He's an ↓excellent ↓↑speaker. (But does he have any new ideas?)

B: I ↓know what you ↓↑mean. (But I'm not sure you are being fair. He has some good ideas.)

In this example, the fall–rise is used to indicate that "more can be said."

2.13 ⊚ CD2 – 58 **Listen and compare the speakers' intonation in a) and b). Which one would you generally expect of an offer of help?**

a) Can I ↑help you?

b) Can I ↓↑help you? (a more polite and friendly offer)

2.14 ⊚ CD2 – 59 **Finally, consider the function of the fall–rise in the following:**

A: We need to improve the ↓**technology**.

B: But training is just as important as ↓↑**technology**.

A: That's just your ↓**opinion**.

B: It's not just an ↓↑**opinion**. There's evidence to support it.

Here, the fall–rise is used by speaker B to indicate a viewpoint that is in some way different from speaker A's.

Unit Summary

In this unit, you have focused on the correct pronunciation of consonant clusters at the end of words and across two words. You have also looked at how intonation is used to organize and emphasize information.

1   **Complete the summary below, using your own words.**

Consonant clusters

● Sometimes, consonant sounds can disappear when

_____

_____

e.g., _____

● -*ed* past forms of regular verbs can be pronounced in three different ways:

_____

_____

e.g., _____

● If you find consonant clusters difficult to pronounce, try

_____

_____

e.g., _____

2 ☉ **CD2 – 60 Listen to the dialogue and mark the rising and falling tones on the stressed words marked in bold.**

A: We need to discuss your **essay**. Can you come to my office at **3.00**?

B: I've got a lecture at **3.00**. And I think I'm working in the **evening**.

A: How about **tomorrow**? I'll be there at **lunchtime**.

B: OK. I'll come **then**.

3 **Think about what you have learned about pronunciation while studying this book and try to answer the questions below.**

a) Which aspects of English pronunciation have you become more aware of while working through this book?

b) How has this helped you when you listen to English speakers?

c) Which aspects of your own pronunciation have you worked on and/or improved most?

d) What sort of tasks and exercises have you found most useful?

e) Which aspects of your pronunciation are you still concerned about?

f) What can you do to continue to work on these areas?

For web resources, see:

www.englishforacademicstudy.com/us/student/pronunciation/links

These weblinks will provide you with further practice in areas of pronunciation such as the sounds, stress, and intonation patterns of English.

g Glossary

Academic Word List (AWL)
A list of 570 word families that are most commonly used in academic contexts.

Connected speech
The stream of words that form the normal pattern of spoken language. It is important to note that words are pronounced differently in connected speech than when they are in isolation.

Consonant
A speech sound made by blocking or partly blocking the air used to make the sound, e.g., blocked /b/ or partly blocked (through the nose) /ŋ/.

Consonant clusters
Groups of consonants that occur together at the beginning, in the middle of, or at the end of words, e.g., _grow_, _congratulate_, _tracks_.

Diphthong
A sound that involves two vowels joined together, e.g., the /aɪ/ sound in _why_. A diphthong is treated as one sound and given a single phonemic symbol.

Falling tone/falling intonation
A downward change in tone (or pitch) that gives the listener more understanding of what the speaker is saying. A falling tone generally indicates finality and certainty, and is often used when the speaker is giving new information.

Function words
Words that have no concrete meaning, but convey grammatical relationships between words, e.g., articles, conjunctions, prepositions.

General Service List (GSL)
The 2,000 most frequently used words in English.

Intonation
The way a speaker raises and lowers her/his tone of voice (or pitch) to clarify meaning. Intonation is used to show attitude or emotion and to clarify discourse and grammatical features.

Micro-skills
Skills that enable the learner to piece together small pieces of information to build a bigger picture and make sense of something. A study of pronunciation helps to develop listening and speaking micro-skills.

Phonemic alphabet
A written set of symbols used to represent the sounds of individual languages.

Phonemic symbol
A symbol that is used to represent an individual sound. The main sounds of English are represented by 44 phonemic symbols.

Phonemic transcription
The use of phonemic symbols to show the sounds of speech in written form. It provides the student with an indication of how a native speaker would pronounce a word, or longer stretches of speech.

Pronunciation
The way sounds are produced to form speech; it covers the individual sounds, the way some sounds are stressed, and the intonation patterns within utterances.

Rising tone/rising intonation

An upward change in tone (or pitch) that gives the listener more understanding of what the speaker is saying. A rising tone generally indicates that the topic or utterance is unfinished, or that the speaker is referring to shared information that has already been introduced.

Sentence stress

The way certain words in a sentence are spoken with more force, also called *prominence*.

Sound/spelling patterns

The connection between the sounds of a language and the way they are spelled. English does not have a one-on-one relationship between sounds and spelling, but there are many useful patterns that will help the speaker.

Suffix

A letter or group of letters that can be added to the end of a word to change its meaning. Words with similar suffixes often have similar stress patterns. Suffixes that come at the end of adjectives include ~*tial*, ~*cial* and ~*ical*.

Syllable

A unit of sound within a word. Each syllable has a vowel at its center, and consonants may "surround" the vowel. It is also possible to have a syllable with just a vowel. For example, one-syllable words: *post*, *take*, two-syllable words: *o•mit, pro•vide, ques•tion*.

Tone unit

A stretch of spoken language that includes at least one prominent syllable that marks the beginning of a change in intonation pattern.

Unvoiced consonant

When pronouncing unvoiced consonants, the vocal chords in your throat do not vibrate, e.g., /p/, /t/ and /k/.

Voiced consonant

When pronouncing voiced consonants, the vocal chords in your throat vibrate, e.g., /b/, /d/ and /g/.

Vowel

A speech sound made without blocking the air used to produce the sound. Variations in vowel sounds are determined mainly by the shape of the mouth, how open the mouth is, and the position of the tongue.

Weak form

When a word changes its pronunciation according to whether it is stressed or not, the unstressed version is known as a weak form. Using a weak form affects the vowel sounds within the word, e.g., *for* is pronounced /fə/ in a weak form.

Word family

A group of words that have the same basic form and similar meanings. For example, the words *produce*, *product*, *production* and *unproductive* are all in the same word family.

Word stress

This is the way that one syllable in a word is given more force. Stressed syllables are louder and longer than unstressed syllables.

Transcripts

Unit 1: Vowel Sounds 1, Word Stress
and Weak Forms

⊕CD1, Track 1

Ex 1.1
Listen to the difference in the pronunciation of
these pairs of words. In each of them, the vowel
sound is different.

a)

fit	feet
dip	deep
hit	heat

b)

mass	mess
band	bend
had	head

c)

hat	heart
match	march
pack	park

d)

ten	turn
head	heard
went	weren't

⊕CD1, Track 2

Ex 1.2
You will hear some of the words from Ex 1.1.
Listen and circle the phonemic transcription that
matches the pronunciation of the word you hear.

Example: heard

a) park
b) turn
c) mass
d) heat
e) weren't
f) deep
g) head
h) heart
i) band

⊕CD1, Track 3

Ex 1.3
Listen to six more words and do the following
exercises.

a) Listen and circle the phonemic transcription
that matches the pronunciation of the word
you hear.

1 seat
2 met
3 hurt
4 fur
5 live
6 sad

⊕CD1, Track 4

Ex 2.1
Listen to these examples of words with one, two,
and three or more syllables.

a) one-syllable words

aid
quote
source
fee

b) two-syllable words

credit
accept
heavy
equate

c) words with three or more syllables

policy
similar
environment
identify
individual

⊕CD1, Track 5

Ex 2.2
Listen to these words and decide how many syllables there are in each of them.

a) specific

b) alter

c) resource

d) preliminary

e) available

f) consequent

g) framework

h) significant

i) adapt

j) differentiate

⊕CD1, Track 6

Ex 3.1
Listen for the stressed syllable in these words.

policy

similar

environment

identify

individual

assume

major

overseas

operation

reinforce

⊕CD1, Track 7

Ex 3.2
Listen again to the words from Ex 2.2. Mark the stressed syllables as shown in the following example.

a) specific

b) alter

c) resource

d) preliminary

e) available

f) consequent

g) framework

h) significant

i) adapt

j) differentiate

⊕CD1, Track 8

Ex 3.3
Listen to the following sentences and mark the stressed syllable in the words in bold.

a) The **protection** of children is the main purpose of this legislation.

b) The samples were **analyzed** in the lab.

c) Chemical **analysis** of the rock provided surprising results.

d) The aim of the study was to **identify** the **factors** contributing to domestic violence.

e) **Periodicals** are kept in an area on the ground floor.

f) The **administration** of these drugs needs to be closely monitored.

g) In **percentage** terms, this is not a significant increase.

h) This is the standard **procedure** for limiting spread of the disease.

⊕CD1, Track 9

Ex 4.1
Listen to these pairs of sentences. What is the difference in the pronunciation of the words in bold in each pair? How can you explain this difference?

a) 1 Interest rates **are** rising. (weak form)

   2 No, that's not true. We **are** doing something about it. (strong form)

b) 1 Would you like **some** tea? (weak form)

   2 Most scientists are convinced about global warming, but **some** are not. (strong form)

c) 1 Where's he coming **from**? (strong form)

   2 Results differed **from** one region to another. (weak form)

d) 1 Is that **your** pen or mine? (strong form)

   2 Can I borrow **your** dictionary? (weak form)

⊕CD1, Track 10

Ex 4.2
Listen to these sentences and write in the missing words, which are all weak forms of function words.

a) One criticism leveled at the board was their lack of financial control.

b) This issue was discussed at some length during the conference.

c) These points should have been made more effectively.

d) How do we account for this change in behavior?

e) This might do more harm than good.

f) This kind of restructuring is usually regarded by employees as a change for the worse.

g) This problem can easily be solved at minimal cost.

h) Trade sanctions will be imposed with effect from the 1st of December.

⊕CD1, Track 11

Ex 4.3
Study the following introduction to a lecture on globalization. Then listen and write in the missing words, which again are weak forms of function words.

Well, as Ros said, I'm going to talk about globalization today, which is one of the catch phrases or buzzwords, if you like, of the late 20th and early 21st centuries. It's constantly in the news. It's used by politicians, by people in the media, by business people, and when they're referring to globalization they talk about things like the way we can communicate almost instantaneously nowadays with people on the other side of the world by e-mail or by telephone. They're also talking about, for example, the way that a fall in share prices in one part of the world, for example in the Far East, can have an immediate impact on the stock markets on the other side of the world, like in London or Frankfurt.

⊕CD1, Track 12

Ex 4.4
Listen to these phrases and repeat them. Can you identify and produce the weak forms of the function words?

a) past and present figures
b) more or less fifty
c) they were selected at random
d) it was far from clear
e) the results of the trials
f) too good to be true
g) needless to say
h) it's gone from bad to worse
i) we'll have to wait and see
j) we had some problems

Unit 1 Summary

⊕CD1, Track 13

Ex 2
Now listen to the words from Ex 1 and mark the stressed syllable in each word.

globalization

century

constantly

politician

refer

media

financial

market

Unit 2: Vowel Sounds 2, Word Stress Patterns

⊕CD1, Track 14

Ex 1.1
Listen to the difference in the pronunciation of these pairs of words. In each of them, the vowel sound is different.

a)

match	much
lack	luck
ankle	uncle

b)

pull	pool
soot	suit
full	fool

c)

spot	sport
shot	short
stock	stork

d)

lock	look
box	books
shock	shook

⊕CD1, Track 15

Ex 1.2
You will hear some of the words from Ex 1.1. Listen and circle the phonemic transcription that matches the pronunciation of the word you hear.

Example: lack

a) books
b) pool
c) spit
d) match
e) uncle
f) fool
g) luck
h) stock
i) short

⊕CD1, Track 16

Ex 1.3
Listen to six more words and do the following exercises.

a) **Listen and circle the phonemic transcription that matches the pronunciation of the word you hear.**

1 fun
2 mud
3 cool
4 bought
5 foot
6 card

◉CD1, Track 17

Ex 2.1
Listen to these examples.

appear
suggest
effort
color

◉CD1, Track 18

Ex 2.2
c) Listen and repeat the words.

Example: computer

1 affect
2 several
3 standard
4 failure
5 purpose
6 propose
7 author
8 attempt
9 distance
10 accept
11 opposite
12 flavour
13 compare
14 approach

◉CD1, Track 19

Ex 2.3
Listen to these examples.

describe
prefer

◉CD1, Track 20

Ex 2.4
c) Listen and repeat the words.

Example: reduce

1 invited
2 decision
3 demand
4 beyond

5 extensive
6 research
7 interpret

◉CD1, Track 21

Ex 3.1
Listen and repeat the following words, making sure you stress the syllables in the columns highlighted in the tables below.

Nouns ending in ~sion or ~tion

discussion
solution
occasion
definition
decision
position

Nouns ending in ~graphy

geography
biography
photography

Adjectives ending in ~ic

electric
economic
specific

Nouns ending in ~ency or ~ancy

frequency
consultancy
consistency
vacancy
efficiency
redundancy

Nouns ending in ~ium

medium
uranium
consortium

Adjectives ending in ~ical

electrical
political
periodical

Nouns ending in ~ity

identity
authority
community

Adjectives ending in ~tial or ~cial

essential
financial
potential
commercial
residential
artificial

Verbs ending in ~ify

modify
clarify
identify

Nouns ending in ~logy

apology
technology
biology

Adjectives ending in ~tional

additional
international
optional

⊛CD1, Track 22

Ex 3.2
b) Listen to check your answers. Repeat the words to practice your pronunciation.

1 academic
2 dimension
3 beneficial
4 similarity
5 majority
6 initial
7 demography
8 allergic
9 tradition
10 deficiency
11 conventional
12 justify

⊛CD1, Track 23

Ex 3.3
Now listen to check your answers.

a) Most of the course units are mandatory, but there are two optional units.

b) The committee hasn't made a decision whether or not to award funding for the project.

c) It's important to start with a definition of the term "sustainable development", as it clearly means different things to different people.

d) Although solar power provides a potential answer to some of the world's energy needs, at the moment the technology is quite expensive.

e) Have we really found a solution to the problem?

f) It's hoped that the development of artificial intelligence will mean that computers will be able to think in the way humans do.

g) There's a lot of confusion, so it's essential to clarify the situation.

h) The stadium was built by an international consortium of construction companies.

i) There's a vacancy for a laboratory technician, so the post will be advertised next week.

j) James Watson's biography of Margaret Thatcher was published last month.

k) The organization plans to publish a new periodical, with three issues a year.

l) Despite plans for economic growth of five percent over the next year, unemployment is continuing to rise.

m) We'll need to modify the design of the equipment after a number of weaknesses were discovered in the testing process.

n) Professor Jones is a leading authority on 17th-century Italian literature.

o) The residential areas of the new town will be located well away from the industrial and commercial zones.

⊛CD1, Track 24

Ex 4.1
Listen to the following examples.

possess	possession	possessive
persuade	persuasion	persuasive
assess	assessment	assessed

However, in some cases the word stress may vary from one form to another. For example:

analyze, analysis, analytical

⊛CD1, Track 25

Ex 4.2
Listen and repeat these words. Mark the stressed syllable. The first one is done for you.

apply	application	applicable
activate	activity	active
inform	information	informative
-	probability	probable
socialize	society	social
experiment	experiment	experimental
equal	equality	equal
unite	union	united
transfer	transfer	transferable

⊛CD1, Track 26

Ex 4.3
Listen to these examples.

occur	occurrence
assume	assumption

⊕CD1, Track 27

Ex 4.5
Listen to the sentences and correct any that you got wrong.

Example: We need to analyze the data.

Statistical analysis of the data provided some unexpected results.

You need good analytical skills for this kind of work.

1 The stomach produces acids, which help to digest food.

   The new model should be in production in November.

   If the factory doesn't become more productive, it faces closure.

   The product was withdrawn from sale after a number of defects were identified.

2 Four alternate methods of payment are offered.

   She takes a very methodical approach to her work.

   They've been developing a new method for research in this area.

3 The president stated that economic development was the main priority.

   The dean is concerned that the economy is overheating.

   She is studying economics at Georgetown University.

4 Wages tend to be higher in the private sector.

   This law is intended to protect people's privacy.

   The water services industry was privatized in the 1980s.

5 The heights of plants varied from 8 cm to 15 cm.

   A wide variety of fruit is grown on the island.

   Regional variations in the unemployment rate are significant.

   A number of variables, such as wind speed and direction, humidity and air pressure, need to be considered.

6 Both approaches yielded similar results.

   There are many similarities between the two religions.

   The firefighters resorted to industrial action to settle the dispute. Similarly, railway workers are threatening to strike because of changes in working practices.

Unit 2 Summary

⊕CD1, Track 28

Ex 1
Listen to the words in the box. Then match them to the phonemic transcriptions below.

other   ankle   pull   shot   uncle   pool
short   another

Unit 3: Consonant Sounds 1, Sentence Stress

⊕CD1, Track 29

Ex 1.1
Listen and repeat these continuous sounds.

sssssssssssssssss

zzzzzzzzzzzzzz

⊕CD1, Track 30

Ex 1.2
Listen and repeat each pair of words. Can you hear the difference in pronunciation?

pie	buy
town	down
coal	goal
sink	zinc
mesh	measure
chunk	junk
fast	vast
breath	breathe

⊕CD1, Track 31

Ex 1.3
Look at the following pairs of words and circle the word you hear.

Example: bill

a) paste
b) symbol
c) dense
d) try
e) wide
f) guard
g) class
h) angle
i) zone
j) price
k) use (v)
l) advise
m) rich
n) badge
o) view
p) prove
q) belief

⊕CD1, Track 32

Ex 1.4
Listen and complete these sentences or phrases.

a) 1 a tense situation
    2 a dense material

b) 1 a wide area
    2 as white as a sheet

c) 1 at the base of the plant
    2 the pace of change

d) 1 Public services have improved.
    2 A cube has six surfaces.

e) 1 difficult to refuse
    2 It's had good reviews.

f) 1 the cause of the fire
    2 It changed the course of his life.

⊕CD1, Track 33

Ex 2.1
Listen to the difference in pronunciation between these pairs of words.

thing	sing
path	pass
worth	worse
mouth	mouse
youth	use
thin	tin
thank	tank
thread	tread
both	boat
death	debt

⊕CD1, Track 34

Ex 2.2
You will hear some of the words from Ex 2.1. Circle the phonemic transcription that matches the pronunciation of the word you hear.

Example: thin

a) tank
b) death
c) both
d) worth
e) pass
f) mouth
g) use

⊕CD1, Track 35

Ex 2.4
Now listen to the correct answers and repeat the sentences.

a) The painting is supposed to be worth five million dollars.

b) The fuel is stored in a 30-liter tank.

c) Cancer is the leading cause of death among women.

d) A thin layer of plastic is needed to provide waterproofing.

e) I couldn't follow the thread of his argument.

f) The thing is, no one likes to be criticized.

g) Tax increases are necessary to finance the national debt.

⊕CD1, Track 36

Ex 3.1
Listen and repeat these words.

the
this
these
that
those
they
their
there
theirs
than
then
though

⊕CD1, Track 37

Ex 3.2
Listen to these sentences and phrases and repeat them.

a) What's the weather like there?
b) Let's get together.
c) I'd rather not.
d) I wouldn't bother.
e) I don't like them.
f) I don't like them, either.
g) … further down the road …
h) … the other day …

⊕CD1, Track 38

Ex 4.1
Listen to these two words.

thank
than

⊙CD1, Track 39

Ex 4.2
Listen to these phrases and write in the correct symbols above the words.

Example: … another thing to consider is …

a) … in theory …
b) … the truth is that …
c) … the growth rate …
d) … a further theme …
e) … they thought that …
f) … this method …
g) … beneath the surface …
h) … this therapy might be used to …
i) … youth culture …

⊙CD1, Track 40

Ex 5.1
Listen to this recording of the previous paragraph.

While word stress (or accent) is generally decided by language rules, sentence stress (or prominence) is decided by speaker choice. The speaker usually chooses to stress content words, which carry the information, and not structure or function words, such as auxiliary verbs, pronouns, prepositions, and determiners, although this is not always the case.

⊙CD1, Track 41

Ex 5.2
Listen to these sentences, in which the sentence stress changes according to the meaning.

You have to hand in the essay on Monday … there's a strict deadline.

You have to hand in the essay on Monday … not the report.

You have to hand in the essay on Monday … not Wednesday.

⊙CD1, Track 42

Ex 5.3
Listen to these beginnings of sentences and choose the more suitable ending, according to the sentence stress.

a) Well, we know how this happened, …
b) Having looked at the effect of deforestation on the environment, …
c) Most of our cotton is imported, …
d) The crime rate fell by 15 percent last year, …
e) The oil pump needs replacing, …

⊙CD1, Track 43

Ex 5.4
Now listen to the complete sentences to check your answers.

a) Well, we know how this happened, but do we know why it happened?
b) Having looked at the effect of deforestation on the environment, we will now discuss greenhouse gases and the roles they play.
c) Most of our cotton is imported, but we produce about 500,000 tonnes a year.
d) The crime rate fell by 15 percent last year, but this year it's risen.
e) The oil pump needs replacing, not the filter.

⊙CD1, Track 44

Ex 5.5
Read and listen to an extract from a lecture called *Introduction to British Agriculture*. Underline the words you hear stressed.

As a backdrop to all these activities, particularly after the Second World War, a lot of effort was put into research and development of agriculture in terms of plant breeding, breeding crops that were higher yielding, that were perhaps disease-resistant, and so on and so forth. Also, crops that might have better quality, better bread-making quality, higher gluten content, to make them doughy, higher protein content, and so on and so forth. Research, too, and this is again at one of the university farms, research into livestock production. Understanding how to better manage our livestock, again to make them produce more, certainly, but also to produce and influence the quality of the livestock products, whether that happens to be milk or cheese, come back to that in a moment, or indeed meat.

⊙CD1, Track 45

Ex 5.7
Read and listen to part of a lecture on globalization. Underline the words you hear stressed.

Now to get to the meat of the lecture, the basic purpose of this lecture is to give you some overview of the kind of contemporary academic and policy debate about globalization and particularly about a very specific, although rather general, debate itself, that's the debate on the effect of globalization on the role of the state. So, you see on the overhead, the lecture's going to be kind of in two parts: the first will be looking at globalization, causes and consequences, and more particularly a kind of definition of the discussion of some of the competing concepts of globalization, that is, you know, what people say it is, so that we can then discuss in some detail, hopefully, this question of how globalization is affecting the state.

Unit 3 Summary

⊕CD1, Track 46

Ex 3
Listen and compare your ideas with the recording.

a) Some species of shark attack people, but most are harmless.
b) There used to be a Chemistry Department, but it closed in 2006.
c) The aid provided to the victims was too little, too late.
d) Many banks stopped lending, when the government wanted them to lend more.

Unit 4: Consonant Sounds 2, Word Stress on Two-Syllable Words

⊕CD1, Track 47

Ex 1.1
Listen to the pronunciation of the words in the box and write them under the correct heading.

decision

version

dimension

occasion

conclusion

discussion

expression

admission

expansion

supervision

confusion

erosion

⊕CD1, Track 48

Ex 1.2
Listen to the three different pronunciations of the word endings in the box and write them under the correct heading.

measure

pressure

closure

assure

ensure

pleasure

leisure

exposure

⊕CD1, Track 49

Ex 1.3
Listen and repeat the following words.

visual

casual

usually

sensual

⊕CD1, Track 50

Ex 2.1
Listen to and repeat the following words and phrases.

visit

develop

value

average

village

very good service

violent

every level

voice

When does it arrive?

⊕CD1, Track 51

Ex 3.1
The /ʝ/ sound appears at the beginning of words starting with *y~*. Listen and repeat.

yet

young

yellow

year

yesterday

⊕CD1, Track 52

Ex 3.2
The /ʝ/ sound also appears at the beginning of some words starting with *u~*. Check the words below that are pronounced /juː~/.

a) union
b) unless
c) uniform
d) uncle
e) unclear
f) unusual
g) useful
h) username
i) usual
j) uranium
k) until
l) urgent

⊕CD1, Track 53

Ex 3.3
You also find the /ʝ/ sound in the middle of words, represented by *y*. Listen to these examples.

beyond

layer

layout

buyer

⊕CD1, Track 54

Ex 3.4
Sometimes, the /ʝ/ sound in the middle of words is not represented by any character. Listen to these words and mark the position of the /ʝ/ sound in them.

Examples:

continue

computer

a) fuel

b) view

c) argue

d) cube

e) few

f) rescue

g) distribute

⊕CD1, Track 55

Ex 4.1
Listen to the difference in pronunciation between these pairs of words.

ship   chip

shop   chop

share   chair

shoes   choose

cash   catch

washed   watched

dishes   ditches

⊕CD1, Track 56

Ex 4.2
You will hear some of the words from Ex 4.1. Circle the phonemic transcription that matches the pronunciation of the word you hear.

Example: chop

a) catch

b) shoes

c) watched

d) share

e) ditches

f) chip

⊕CD1, Track 57

Ex 4.4
Listen to the correct answers and repeat the sentences.

a) There's a small chip on the card that stores your personal data.

b) You can pay with cash or by check.

c) Farmers need to dig ditches to drain the soil.

d) The share value has shot up by 30 percent!

e) You can choose which topic to write about for your assignment.

f) The sample should be washed in a five percent saline solution before analysis.

⊕CD1, Track 58

Ex 5.1
Listen to the difference in pronunciation between these pairs of words.

chunk   junk

cheap   Jeep

H   age

search   surge

rich   ridge

batch   badge

⊕CD1, Track 59

Ex 5.2
You will hear some of the words from Ex 5.1. Circle the phonemic transcription that matches the pronunciation of the word you hear.

Example: search

a) ridge

b) age

c) chunk

d) batch

e) Jeep

⊕CD1, Track 60

Ex 5.4
Listen to the correct answers and repeat the sentences.

a) Most fruit and vegetables are rich in vitamins.

b) Credit card bills are generally prepared by batch processing of data.

c) A large chunk of the budget is spent on overheads.

d) There's a ridge of high pressure running from north-west to south-east.

e) Children today eat too much junk food.

f) A sudden surge in the power supply can damage your computer.

⊕CD1, Track 61

Ex 6.1
Put the words into the correct column, according to their stress pattern.

provide

system

assist

reason

prepare

appear

recent

receive

include

certain

factor

question

problem

modern

suggest

reduce

private

observe

⊕CD1, Track 62

Ex 6.2
Listen to these pairs of sentences and underline the syllable that is stressed in the words in bold.

Example:

Coffee is this country's biggest export.

They export coffee mainly to Europe.

a) There's been a significant increase in unemployment.

It's been decided to increase the interest rate by a quarter of a percent.

b) You need to keep a record of all the references you use in the essay.

She wants to record the lecture with her MP3 player.

c) About 30 people were present at the seminar.

He plans to present the results of his research at the conference.

⊕CD1, Track 63

Ex 6.4
Unlike the two-syllable words in Ex 6.3, the stress in words ending in ~er, ~ry, ~le, ~ion, ~age, ~ish, ~ow and ~us generally falls on the first syllable. Listen and repeat these words.

answer

gather

matter

suffer

angry

hurry

story

vary

angle

handle

middle

trouble

action

mention

nation

question

damage

language

manage

package

English

finish

publish

rubbish

follow

narrow

shadow

window

focus

minus

Unit 4 Summary

⊕CD1, Track 64

Ex 3
Listen to the following pairs of sentences, which contain words in bold with the same spelling. Mark the stressed syllable in each pair of words. For which pairs is the word stress the same, and for which is it different?

a) The contracts were signed last week.

The metal contracts as it cools down.

b) It caused a lot of damage.

How does it damage your health?

c) Why did they object to the proposal?

Archaeologists aren't sure what this object was used for.

d) What's the main focus of your research?

We need to focus on the real issues.

Unit 5: Diphthongs 1, Sounds in Connected Speech

⊕CD2, Track 1

Ex 1.1
Put the words in the box into the correct column, according to the pronunciation of the vowel or diphthong sound.

time

think

life

write

while

win

high

try

sit

site

buy

bit

might

sign

like

⊕CD2, Track 2

Ex 1.3
How do you pronounce *L-I-V-E* in each of these sentences?

a) Where do you live?

b) The match is being shown live on TV.

⊕CD2, Track 3

Ex 1.4
Listen to the six words below and complete the two activities.

a) Circle the phonemic transcription that matches the pronunciation of the word you hear.

1 while

2 fit

3 style

4 height

5 litter

6 hide

⊕CD2, Track 4

Ex 1.5
Underline the /aɪ/ sounds in these sentences or phrases. Then listen and repeat them.

a) Try the other side.

b) The height's fine.

c) This type of plant needs a lot of light.

d) There was a slight rise in the share value.

⊕CD2, Track 5

Ex 2.1
Put the words in the box into the correct column, according to the pronunciation of the vowel or diphthong sound.

cost

coast

show

rod

road

grow

lot

load

flow

hope

code

cold

not

note

fold

⊕CD2, Track 6

Ex 2.3
Listen to the six words below and complete the activities.

a) Listen and circle the phonemic transcription that matches the pronunciation of the word you hear.

1 coast

2 not

3 rod

4 soak

5 won't

6 fond

⊕CD2, Track 7

Ex 2.4
Underline the /oʊ/ sounds in these sentences or phrases. Then listen and repeat.

a) Most of the gold is exported.

b) … the hole in the ozone layer …

c) Gross profits were down.

d) Can you cope with the workload?

⦿CD2, Track 8

Ex 3.1
Put the words in the box into the correct column, according to the pronunciation of the vowel or diphthong sound.

plan

plane

dark

face

make

scale

large

lack

heart

play

weigh

gain

part

claim

bad

⦿CD2, Track 9

Ex 3.3
Listen to the eight words below and complete the activities.

a) Circle the phonemic transcription that matches the pronunciation of the word you hear.

    1 lack

    2 tape

    3 plan

    4 latter

    5 aim

    6 mark

    7 pace

    8 came

⦿CD2, Track 10

Ex 3.4
Underline the /eɪ/ sounds in these sentences or phrases. Then listen and repeat.

a) Can you explain this heavy rainfall?

b) That's quite a claim to make.

c) The future remains uncertain.

d) The failure rate is quite high.

⦿CD2, Track 11

Ex 4.1
Listen to these short conversations.

a) What do we need to solve the problem? A system.

b) What would you like me to do? Assist him.

⦿CD2, Track 12

Ex 4.2
Listen to the following examples.

hand in

split up

complex issue

⦿CD2, Track 13

Ex 4.3
Listen to these phrases and repeat them, linking the words together where this is indicated.

a) divide‿in two

b) historical‿evidence

c) as soon‿as possible

d) take‿over control

e) it'll‿end next week

f) the Data Protection‿Act

g) a wide‿area

h) keep‿up with‿it

i) an‿increase‿in crime

j) the main‿aim

⦿CD2, Track 14

Ex 4.4
Listen to this introduction from a talk about home ownership and write in the links between words.

In this presentation I'm going to talk about home ownership in the UK. First I'm going to focus on changes in the patterns of home ownership in the last 20 years and provide an explanation for these changes. Then I'm going to describe the process of buying or selling a house. Finally I'm going to try to make some predictions about the housing market.

⦿CD2, Track 15

Ex 4.6
Listen to the following examples.

slow economic growth

true identity

go up

⦿CD2, Track 16

Ex 4.7
Listen to the following examples.

carry on

high altitude

free access

⦿CD2, Track 17

Ex 4.8

Listen to the following examples.

aware of the problem

after all

faster access

⊛CD2, Track 18

Ex 4.9
Listen to these phrases and decide if a /w/, /j/ or /r/ sound needs to be inserted.

a) try out

b) agree on this

c) two of them

d) driver error

e) radio operator

f) high above the Earth

g) How does this tie in?

Unit 5 Summary

⊛CD2, Track 19

Ex 1
Underline the diphthong sounds /aɪ/ in sentence (a), /oʊ/ in sentence (b) and /eɪ/ in sentence (c).

a) I think I'd like to carry on with Life Sciences, but I'm also interested in Psychology.

b) I want to go into social work, so I'm studying Sociology.

c) He came to Boston to present a paper on International Relations.

Unit 6: Consonant Clusters 1, Tone Units 1

⊛CD2, Track 20

Ex 1.1
Listen and repeat these groups of words, which begin with consonant clusters.

blame
blind
blood

brand
break
brief

draw
draft
drop

platform
plenty
plus

practice
pressure
profit

transaction
trend
trigger

claim
climate
closure

create
crucial
criteria

quarter
quality
quota

glass
global
glue

graphics
ground
growth

twelve
twice
twin

flexible
flight
flow

fraction
freeze
frequent

threat
through
throw

shrink
shred

⊛CD2, Track 21

Ex 1.2
Listen and complete these sentences.

a) It burns with a blue flame.

b) There was a gradual rise in crime.

c) We are on track for ten percent growth this year.

d) We need a more precise definition of the term.

e) It's covered with a steel plate.

f) The drum needs to be replaced.

g) Its development can be traced back to the 15th century.

h) The screen went blank.

i) There's fresh evidence for such a link.

j) It's difficult to follow the thread of his argument.

⊛CD2, Track 22

Ex 1.4
Listen and repeat these further examples of consonant clusters that begin with /s/.

scale
scheme
scope
score

screen
script

snack
snow

sleep
slip
slight
slope

smart
smell
smoke
smooth

spare
spill
speed
spoil
specific

spray
spread
spring

split
splendid

stage
step
store
stuff
style

straight
stress
strike
strong

sweet
swing
switch

⊛CD2, Track 23

Ex 1.5
Listen and complete these phrases or sentences.

a)   This machine scans the brain.

b)   Resources are scarce.

c)   This species is under threat.

d)   We're making slow progress.

e)   one important strategy

f)   He splashed paint on the floor.

g)   a strange feeling

h)   a bigger slice of the cake

i)   in a stable condition

j)   a stone floor

⊛CD2, Track 24

Ex 2.1
Listen and repeat these words, which include consonant clusters.

impress
comprise
compromise

complain
complete
employ
sample

central
contract
control
entry
introduce

inspect
transport

explain
exploit
explore
explicit

extract
extreme

include
conclude
enclose
unclear

conflict
influence
inflation

abstract
construct
distribute
industry
illustrate

⊛CD2, Track 25

Ex 2.2
Listen and complete these phrases or sentences with words from Ex 2.1.

a)   Supplies need to be distributed.

b)   no explicit reference

c)   the transport infrastructure

d)   this conflicts with

e)   The causes are unclear.

f)   oils extracted from plants

g)   an abstract concept

h)   in order to exploit its potential fully

i)   It comprises three parts.

j)   in extreme cases

CD2, Track 26

Ex 3.1
Listen to these sentences and write in the word that is missing.

a) Did he tell you?

b) I've added her name to the list.

c) Can you put his suitcase in the car?

CD2, Track 27

Ex 3.2
Listen and complete the sentences.

a) Although they've requested further funding, it's not certain that the project will continue beyond 2015.

b) The treatment is expensive, and that's why it's not very widely available.

c) Another advantage is that it'd lower the costs.

d) In fact, they're supposed to be checked every six months.

e) We can't know for sure, but it's thought that the space probe might've been hit by a meteorite.

f) Unfortunately, I'd forgotten just how complicated the process is.

g) The Vikings are believed to've landed in America well before Columbus.

h) The equipment testing shouldn't've been left until the last minute.

CD2, Track 28

Ex 3.3
Listen to these words and phrases and, in the words in bold, cross out the vowels that are not pronounced.

a) Vegetables are grown on about 60 percent of farms in the area.

b) Perhaps he's left.

c) The laboratory is closed on Sundays.

d) I'll probably be late.

e) He lives a comfortable life.

CD2, Track 29

Ex 3.4
Listen to the sentences a–e, paying particular attention to the consonant clusters in the words in bold. Cross out the consonants that are not pronounced.

a) It reacts with sulphur.

b) They'll send back the results on Tuesday.

c) It must be checked.

d) The low election turnout reflects growing apathy towards politics.

e) The engine tends to overheat in particular circumstances.

CD2, Track 30

Ex 4.1
Listen to someone speaking the above text and notice how it is split into tone units.

Whereas written English is split into words, spoken English is split into what are known as tone units. Each tone unit contains at least one prominent syllable. If, however, it contains two, then it's usually the second that contains the main sentence stress. This is the tonic syllable and it is where most of the pitch change takes place.

CD2, Track 31

Ex 4.2
Listen to part of the lecture entitled *An Introduction to British Agriculture*. Mark the tone units by writing in double slash signs in the right places.

As a backdrop to all these activities, particularly after the Second World War, a lot of effort was put into research and development of agriculture in terms of plant breeding, breeding crops that were higher yielding, that were perhaps disease-resistant, and so on and so forth.

Also, crops that might have better quality, better bread-making quality, higher gluten content to make them doughy, higher protein content, and so on and so forth.

Research, too, and this is again at one of the university farms, research into livestock production.

Understanding how to better manage our livestock, again to make them produce more, certainly, but also to produce and influence the quality of the livestock products, whether that happens to be milk or cheese, come back to that in a moment, or indeed meat.

CD2, Track 32

Ex 4.3
Now listen to an extract from the lecture on globalization. Mark the tone units by writing in double slash signs in the right places.

Now to get to the meat of the lecture, the basic purpose of this lecture is to give you some overview of the kind of contemporary academic and policy debate about globalization and particularly about a very specific, although rather general debate itself, that's the debate on the effect of globalization on the role of the state. So you see on the overhead the lecture's going to be kind of in two parts: the first will be looking at globalization, causes and consequences and more particularly a kind of definition of the discussion of some of the competing concepts of globalization, that is, you know, what people say it is, so that we can then discuss in some detail hopefully this question of how globalization is affecting the state.

Unit 6 Summary

⊕CD2, Track 33

Ex 1
Listen to how the following words are pronounced. Say the words in each group below. Underline any words that you find difficult to pronounce.

a) spare   spoil   speed   spray
b) central entry   quarter track
c) school   scale   share   scheme
d) street   store   stress   straight
e) complete complex construct comprise
f) abstract industry construct inspect

⊕CD2, Track 34

Ex 4
a) Listen to someone speaking the above text and mark the tone units.

You've got some interesting ideas and make some good points, but you could have developed these a little more. You must make sure that you check your essay for spelling mistakes and make sure the grammar is correct. Perhaps you should've asked the graduate assistant to read through your work. He would have helped you improve it.

Unit 7 Diphthongs 2, Tone Units 2

⊕CD2, Track 35

Ex 1.1
Put the words in the box into the correct column of the table, according to the pronunciation of the diphthong sound.

share
fair
mere
square
near
adhere
sphere
year
there
where
aware
appear
severe
wear
pair

chair
bear
fare

⊕CD2, Track 36

Ex 1.3
Using words from Ex 1.1, complete these sentences by writing in the missing words.

a) As far as I'm aware, there's been little previous research into this issue.

b) Patients suffering from severe depression are often treated with drugs.

c) The mere fact that they have agreed to negotiate does not indicate that an end to the conflict is near.

d) These countries needed to prepare for entry into the EMU.

e) How can we repair the damage that has been done?

f) The area of land is about 20 square meters.

g) The seeds adhere to the fur of animals, which distribute them over a large area.

h) We need to bear in mind that events in South America are largely beyond the UK's sphere of influence.

⊕CD2, Track 37

Ex 2.1
Put the words in the box into the correct column of the table, according to the pronunciation of ow.

allow
crowd
below
own
flow
down
power
growth
now
know
slow
follow
brown
show
powder
crown
owe
shower

⊕CD2, Track 38

Ex 2.2
Underline the words below which include the /aʊ/ sound.

loud
doubt
group
account
court
serious
sound
various
trouble
south
amount
color
course
enough
young
hour
ground
flavor

⊕CD2, Track 39

Ex 2.3
Listen and complete the sentences, using words from Exs 2.1 and 2.2.

a) How do we account for this increase in temperature?

b) Margaret Thatcher came to power in 1979.

c) The new road system is designed to improve traffic flow through the city center.

d) The animal feed is usually sold in powder form.

e) It's without doubt the most serious crisis the government has faced.

f) You need to allow 21 days for delivery.

g) Economic growth has slowed down over the last six months.

h) He's doing research into crowd behavior.

i) A significant amount of water is lost through perspiration.

j) The cheese has quite a strong flavor.

⊕CD2, Track 40

Ex 3.1
Listen and repeat the following words.

coin
point
join
avoid
soil
noise
boy
employ
enjoy
royal
annoy
soy

⊕CD2, Track 41

Ex 3.2
Listen and complete these sentences by writing a word in each space.

a) The questionnaire comprises multiple-choice and open questions.

b) The government wants parents to have a voice in determining how their children are educated.

c) During the civil war, the army remained loyal to the king.

d) The company has appointed a new marketing director.

e) Large parts of the city were destroyed in the earthquake.

f) It's often claimed that we fail to exploit scientific developments made in UK universities.

g) Many sailors died during long sea voyages because of poor nutrition.

h) The new company is a joint venture between Italian and Egyptian oil companies.

⊕CD2, Track 42

Ex 4.1
Listen and complete this lecture on higher education in the US. Write one to five words in each space.

... in the US, but in order to do that I'm going to tell you something about the education system before students get to the higher level. There are several reasons for this. One is, of course, it's part of the plan of your course designers to give you the experience of lectures before you go into your real departments in September, but another reason is that we've found in the past that many students come to the US and they live and study here for a year or two and they go away without knowing some of the most basic facts about the education system here. It's also true that the education system here, perhaps as in your countries, is changing very rapidly, and this means that if you ask older people, you know, people as old as me, who don't actually have direct experience, they probably give you information about the education system as it used to be rather than as it actually is now.

Now what qualifications, as it were, do I have to speak on this particular subject? Well, I'm, as was said in the introduction, I'm here at Boston University and my main task is to look after international students here, like you, who need academic language support. Now between 20 and 23 percent of the students in this university, in Boston University, don't have English as their first language and didn't receive their previous education in the United States. So that's a large number of students, that's, you know, almost two thousand five hundred students, in this university who were not actually educated in the United States before they came to the university, so you are among many. You are, you know, a minority, but you're a very large minority.

⊕CD2, Track 43

Ex 4.3
Listen to this excerpt from a lecture titled *Financial Markets and Instruments* and decide where the sentence stress falls.

Well, the title, *Financial Markets and Instruments*, what are we going to do here? Well, we're going to start by explaining why we need a financial market at all. What's the role that is played by a financial market? What's the rationale for having a financial market? And then we're going to move on and explain some of the instruments that are traded in those markets, some of the instruments that I was saying you're familiar with already, because they are simply stocks, bonds, bills: money market instruments. If you've taken any finance courses before, you might be familiar also with the other ones, which are future swap options, which are derivative instruments, and I'm going to focus mainly on the stocks, bonds, bills, since these are by far the easiest to understand. OK, let's start with a simple definition, and I guess anyone here could have given this definition on their own: what's a financial market? Well, a financial market is a market where financial securities are traded. Nothing very tricky here.

Unit 7 Summary

⊕CD2, Track 44

Ex 1
Listen and check your answers.

annoy

square

crowd

growth

severe

soy

although

doubt

steer

owe

pair

south

bear

avoid

year

Unit 8: Consonant Clusters 2, Intonation

⊕CD2, Track 45

Ex 1.1
Listen and repeat these groups of words, which end with consonant clusters.

arrival
critical
external
financial
principal

assemble
resemble

impact
conflict
affect
abstract

range
arrange
change
challenge

criticism
mechanism
organism
tourism

eleven
given
govern
driven

depth
length
strength
width
wealth

branch
lunch
launch
bench

⊕CD2, Track 46

Ex 1.2
Listen to these phrases and sentences and write the missing words in the spaces.

a) in the initial stage

b) The job has some fringe benefits.

c) I've lost a bunch of keys.

d) a rather uneven surface

e) It was discussed at some length.

f) This is a key aspect of his work.

g) He's studying journalism at Leeds University.

h) They can't afford to take such a gamble.

i) the removal of investment controls

j) in the seventh grade

⊕CD2, Track 47

Ex 1.3
Listen to the past verb forms in the box and put them in the correct column of the table, depending on the pronunciation of ~ed.

equipped

combined

involved

concluded

constructed

depended

developed

expressed

claimed

advised

arranged

adapted

lacked

finished

absorbed

⊕CD2, Track 48

Ex 1.4
Listen to the following examples.

I watch television every night.

and

I watched television last night.

or

Many suppliers raise their prices in situations like this.

and

Many suppliers raised their prices when the exchange rate rose.

⊕CD2, Track 49

Ex 1.5
Listen and repeat these phrases.

a) arranged at short notice

b) the team involved in the project

c) it was constructed in three months

d) it's absorbed into the bloodstream

e) the benefits claimed in the report

f) we've avoided the problem

g) a technique developed in Brazil

h) specially adapted equipment

i) aimed at a niche market

j) enclosed in plastic

⊕CD2, Track 50

Ex 2.1
Listen to the following short exchange.

A: Has everything been checked?

B: Yes, I think so.

A: What about the temperature?

B: Yes, I've checked the temperature, and it's normal.

Listen to the two words in isolation.

A: temperature

B: temperature

⊕CD2, Track 51

Ex 2.2
Listen to another short exchange and do the three activities below.

A: It's too expensive.

B: Well, it's expensive, but it's worth it.

⊕CD2, Track 52

Ex 2.3
Compare this conversation with the previous one.

A: It's too expensive.

B: Yes, it's a lot of money, but it's worth it.

⊕CD2, Track 53

Ex 2.4
Listen to these short conversations. Notice the falling intonation for new information and the rising tone for information that is not new.

a) A: When's the deadline for the new building project?

B: The deadline? I think it's next Thursday.

b) A: Why do these prices fluctuate?

B: Changes in the exchange rate cause this variation.

⊕CD2, Track 54

Ex 2.5
Listen to this conversation and mark the falling and rising intonation.

A: Can I help you?

B: Yes, where's the Physics Department?

A: It's on the second floor.

B: On the second floor?

A: Yes, that's right. Take the elevator over there.

B: I don't like elevators. I'd rather walk there.

A: Suit yourself. The stairs are down the hall, on the left.

B: Down there, on the left. Thanks very much!

Ex 2.7
Listen to this short extract from a lecture and think about the use of intonation.

In these two lectures, we're going to look at two theories of child development. First, I'm going to look at Jean Piaget. Then, next week, I'll talk about the life and work of Erick Erickson. So this week, it's about Jean Piaget. Now, Piaget's theories were very much influenced by his own experiences, so I'm going to talk about his life and how he developed his ideas, and then I'm going to describe Piaget's four stages of child development.

⊛CD2, Track 56

Ex 2.9
Listen to a student talking about the advantages and disadvantages of streaming video from a website and mark the rising and falling tones on the stressed words in bold.

With streaming video, the video is downloaded to your computer as you are listening to it. And usually you can't save it.

This stops people from making copies of the video, editing or pirating it.

The problem is, if you don't have enough bandwidth, or if you're on a network and it's very busy, your computer won't be able to download fast enough.

As a result, the picture quality is often poor, or the pictures are jerky. Sometimes, the video even freezes.

⊛CD2, Track 57

Ex 2.12
Listen again to the first dialogue in Ex 2.1.
A: Has everything been checked?
B: Yes, I think so.

Consider also:
A: He's an excellent speaker.
B: I know what you mean.

⊛CD2, Track 58

Ex 2.13
Listen and compare the speakers' intonation in a) and b). Which one would you generally expect of an offer of help?
a) Can I help you?
b) Can I help you?

⊛CD2, Track 59

Ex 2.14
Finally, consider the function of the fall–rise in the following.
A: We need to improve the technology.
B: But training is just as important as technology.
A: That's just your opinion.
B: It's not just an opinion. There's evidence to support it.

Unit 8 Summary

⊛CD2, Track 60

Ex 2
Listen to the dialogue and mark the rising and falling tones on the stressed words marked in bold.
A: We need to discuss your essay. Can you come to my office at three o'clock?
B: I've got a lecture at three o'clock. And I think I'm working in the evening.
A: How about tomorrow? I'll be there at lunchtime.
B: OK. I'll come then.